NEW OBJECTIVE TESTS IN ENGLISH LANGUAGE

NEW OBJECTIVE TESTS IN ENGLISH LANGUAGE

B. Rowe BA
Senior Lecturer in English
Maria Assumpta College of Education
London

R. A. Banks MA PhD
Head of the English Department
Borough Road College
Isleworth, Middlesex

HODDER AND STOUGHTON
LONDON SYDNEY AUCKLAND TORONTO

ISBN 0 340 16230 9

Printed and bound in Great Britain for
Hodder and Stoughton Educational,
a division of Hodder and Stoughton Ltd, London,
by Hazell Watson & Viney Ltd, Aylesbury, Bucks

INTRODUCTION

This book is intended to complement *Objective Tests in English Language for GCE*, which was published in 1970. At that time we were aware that the volume of tests was orientated specifically towards those working in schools, colleges, or privately, for the GCE of those awarding bodies and universities which had introduced multiple-choice objective tests into their examinations in English Language. With the publication of the Schools Council's suggestions for the introduction of a single examination at 16+, and following the schemes under active consideration, it seemed that we should now follow up our earlier work with a book to help those preparing for CSE or other examinations in English. We are grateful to our many colleagues in the teaching profession who urged us to undertake the work.

A book which consists largely of passages and objective tests runs the risk of being used in isolation from the rest of a student's work in English. We are anxious that this should not happen. The passages and the items which follow them will allow and encourage careful analysis and development of response, understanding, and reasoning. Teachers of English are, of course, dealing with such analysis and development in all areas of their work, and we should like the material in this book to provide additional suitable passages for them to use. At the end of each test we have included some suggestions for further work in English arising from the study of the extracts. With the help of these suggestions, which are varied in their form and content, we hope that students will be able to link their examination of the tests themselves with other stimulating and relevant follow-up reading, discussions, project work, essay-writing, and activities. In this way the possible isolation of the study of objective tests from the whole area of English teaching will be avoided and, indeed, this book should help to make such a study the springboard into the deeper consideration of English. The analysis of the central theme of a passage will allow the sensitive student to move out into related areas of work by means of the suggestions we offer.

For those new to multiple-choice objective tests an explanation of their form might prove helpful. The 'questions' which follow each of the passages are known as *items*. Each item consists of a *stem*, which is an introductory question, direction, or incomplete statement, and five suggested answers called the *responses* or *options*. Only one of these options, the *key*, is the correct or best answer to the problem or question posed in the stem; the remaining options, which are incorrect or less appropriate, are called *distractors*. The items are related to important aspects of the subject matter and its presentation and set out to test the student's ability to remember, understand, and think. The options sometimes require him to discriminate between not only right and wrong responses but also the good and the best or the probable and the most probable.

Before the items are attempted it is important that the passage on which they are based should be read several times and its general framework understood. The *key* to each item can be found most easily by (1) reading the *stem* carefully until its requirements are clear and (2) relating the stem to the context to which it refers. The five *options* can then be considered and evaluated and the key (**A, B, C, D,** or **E**) selected. The tests can be quickly marked by reference to the list of answers supplied at the back of the book.

It is important, too, that a student should not try to arrive at the key by guesswork. At one time a formula to allow for guessing was built into the method used by examining bodies to assess the final results in order to eliminate any advantage a candidate might be thought to have gained by guessing correctly, although this procedure is used much less now. If any item seems too difficult, time should not be lost by puzzling over it for too long. It is best to move on to the next and come back to the difficult one later, if time allows.

Each test in this book is designed so that it can be completed within 40 minutes, the amount of time usually available for students to answer a comprehension exercise in class. As an assessment test it is clearly important that the items on a passage should be completed at one sitting within a rigid time-framework, but teachers who prefer to use a test as a basis for discussion will find it very easy to divide the items so that they can spend considerably longer than 40 minutes on a passage and its deeper evaluation.

B. R.
R. A. B.

In the middle of the night I woke from a dream full of whips and lariats as long as serpents, and runaway coaches on mountain passes, and wide, windy gallops over cactus fields, and I heard the man in the next room crying, 'Gee-up!' and 'Whoa!' and trotting his tongue on the roof of his mouth.

5   It was the first time I had stayed in grandpa's house. The floorboards had squeaked like mice as I climbed into bed, and the mice between the walls had creaked like wood as though another visitor was walking on them. It was a mild summer night, but curtains had flapped and branches beaten against the window. I had pulled the sheets over my head, and soon was roaring and
10 riding in a book.

    'Whoa there, my beauties!' cried grandpa. His voice sounded very young and loud, and his tongue had powerful hooves, and he made his bedroom into a great meadow. I thought I would see if he was ill, or had set his bedclothes on fire, for my mother had said that he lit his pipe under the blankets, and had
15 warned me to run to his help if I smelt smoke in the night. I went on tiptoe through the darkness to his bedroom door, brushing against the furniture and upsetting a candlestick with a thump. When I saw there was a light in the room I felt frightened, and as I opened the door I heard grandpa shout, 'Gee-up!' as loudly as a bull with a megaphone.

20   He was sitting up in bed and rocking from side to side as though the bed were on a rough road; the knotted edges of the counterpane were his reins; his invisible horse stood in a shadow beyond the bedside candle. Over a white flannel nightshirt he was wearing a red waistcoat with walnut-sized brass buttons. The over-filled bowl of his pipe smouldered among his whiskers like a
25 little, burning hayrick on a stick. At the sight of me, his hands dropped from the reins and lay blue and quiet, the bed stopped still on a level road, he muffled his tongue into silence, and the horses drew softly up.

    'Is there anything the matter, grandpa?' I asked, though the clothes were not on fire. His face in the candlelight looked like a ragged quilt pinned
30 upright on the black air and patched all over with goat-beards.

    He stared at me mildly. Then he blew down his pipe, scattering the sparks and making a high, wet dog-whistle of the stem, and shouted: 'Ask no questions.'

    After a pause, he said slyly: 'Do you ever have nightmares, boy?'
35   I said: 'No.'

continue overleaf

1

'Oh, yes, you do,' he said.

I said I was woken by a voice that was shouting to horses.

'What did I tell you?' he said. 'You eat too much. Who ever heard of horses in a bedroom?'

40 He fumbled under his pillow, brought out a small tinkling bag, and carefully untied its strings. He put a sovereign in my hand, and said: 'Buy a cake.' I thanked him and wished him good night.

As I closed my bedroom door, I heard his voice crying loudly and gaily, 'Gee-up! gee-up! and the rocking of the travelling bed.

45 [The next day grandpa was missing from his house and so we set out in search of him.]

The trap rattled on to the bridge, and I saw grandpa there: the buttons of his waistcoat shone in the sun, he wore his tight, black Sunday trousers and a tall, dusty hat I had seen in a cupboard in the attic, and he carried an ancient
50 bag. He bowed to us. 'Good morning, Mr Price,' he said, 'and Mr Griff and Mr Morgan and Mr Evans.' To me he said: 'Good morning, boy.'

Mr Griff pointed his coloured stick at him.

'And what do you think you are doing on Carmarthen bridge in the middle of the afternoon,' he said sternly, 'with your best waistcoat and your old hat?'
55 Grandpa did not answer, but inclined his face to the river wind, so that his beard was set dancing and wagging as though he talked, and watched the coracle men move, like turtles, on the shore.

Mr Griff raised his stunted barber's pole. 'And where do you think you are going,' he said, 'with your old black bag?'
60 Grandpa said: 'I am going to Llangadock to be buried.' And he watched the coracle shells slip into the water lightly, and the gulls complain over the fish-filled water as bitterly as Mr Price complained:

'But you aren't dead yet, Dai Thomas.'

For a moment grandpa reflected, then: 'There's no sense in lying dead in
65 Llanstephan,' he said. 'The ground is comfy in Llangadock; you can twitch your legs without putting them in the sea.'

His neighbours moved close to him. They said: 'You aren't dead, Mr Thomas.'

'How can you be buried, then?'
70 'Nobody's going to bury you in Llanstephan.'

'Come on home, Mr Thomas.'

'There's strong beer for tea.'

'And cake.'

But grandpa stood firmly on the bridge, and clutched his bag to his side, and
75 stared at the flowing river and the sky, like a prophet who has no doubt.

Dylan Thomas, 'A Visit to Grandpa's',
Portrait of the Artist as a Young Dog

1 The lariats (line 1) are compared with serpents probably because both are all of the following EXCEPT

    A long
    B thin
    C poisonous
    D stinging
    E coiling

2 The immediate cause of the author's dream of cowboys was most probably

    A a film he had seen
    B his grandfather's cries
    C memories of horse-riding
    D his own early childhood
    E the squeaking of the mice

3 'Squeaked' (line 6) and 'creaked' (line 7) as they are used in the passage both suggest noises which are all of the following EXCEPT

    A mysterious
    B impossible to ignore
    C amusing
    D difficult to distinguish
    E frightening

4 When the writer suggests that grandfather had 'made his bedroom into a great meadow' (lines 12–13) he is indicating that

    A grandfather was trying to get outside
    B the horses were really outside in the field
    C plants in the room suggested it was a field
    D the furniture had been moved round
    E his imagination was creating the scene

5 The author went to his grandfather's bedroom because he

    A wanted to join in the fun he knew would occur
    B thought his grandfather was in danger
    C had just been told by his mother to go
    D believed that his grandfather had a horse there
    E had smelt burning in the middle of the night

6 The night seemed to be all of the following EXCEPT

    A warm
    B humid
    C summery
    D windy
    E dark

continue overleaf

7 All of the following may help to explain the author's fear when he saw the light in his grandfather's room (lines 17–18) EXCEPT that he

A thought the place might be on fire
B feared his grandfather might be ill
C felt someone else had entered the house
D did not feel able to help with a nightmare
E knew his mother would be angry he had got up

8 Which of the following is nearest in meaning to 'megaphone' as it is used in line 19?

A Speaking trumpet
B Giant loudspeaker
C Powerful microphone
D Relay machine
E Enormous gramophone

9 Which of the following is nearest in meaning to 'counterpane' as it is used in line 21?

A Blanket
B Sheet
C Pillow
D Coverlet
E Bolster

10 The horse which 'stood in a shadow beyond the bedside candle' (line 22) was invisible because it was

A hiding
B obscured
C frightened
D imaginary
E ghostly

11 All of the following help to describe the grandfather's appearance in bed EXCEPT that he

A wore a nightshirt and red waistcoat
B was smoking a pipe which was too full
C sat in bed rocking to and fro
D was holding firmly on to the bedclothes
E had a long, straggling, unkempt beard

4

12 The author's first question, 'Is there anything the matter, grandpa?' (line 28 suggests that the boy thought

- **A** he could see flames in the room
- **B** his grandfather was very ill
- **C** there were horses in the room
- **D** this was an act for his benefit
- **E** his own mind was leaving him

13 The description of his grandfather's face as 'a ragged quilt' (line 29) suggests that it

- **A** seemed part of the unkempt bed
- **B** was puffy and screwed up at the seams
- **C** had clearly been worn by age
- **D** was scratched all over in the excitement
- **E** appeared white and patchy in places

14 The pipe's stem is described as a 'dog-whistle' (line 32) because it

- **A** produced a very high-pitched note
- **B** was used to summon animals
- **C** seemed of about the same length
- **D** needed to be cleared by blowing hard
- **E** had a dual-purpose built into it

15 The boy's answer, 'No' (line 35) to his grandfather's question reveals that the boy

- **A** was unable to tell the truth
- **B** wanted to reassure his grandfather
- **C** did not understand the point of the question
- **D** refused to admit his own weakness
- **E** could not accept such nightmares

16 The grandfather's offer to the boy of a sovereign to 'buy a cake' (line 41) suggests in the context all of the following EXCEPT that he

- **A** did not understand the value of money
- **B** hoped to buy off the boy's suspicions
- **C** wanted the boy to continue to like him
- **D** thought he was still driving his coach
- **E** wished the boy to have nightmares too

continue overleaf

17 Mr Griff spoke 'sternly' (line 54) to grandpa because he

    A had wasted his afternoon in the search
    B wanted to bring the old man to his senses
    C feared he would get no reply otherwise
    D imagined he was important as leader of the party
    E expected the old man was about to attack him

18 'Coracle-men' (line 57) were

    A dockers unloading a coal ship at the dock-side
    B small, stunted men who moved with difficulty
    C shore-fishermen attending to their lines
    D beachcombers searching for what they could find
    E owners of small, skin-covered boats used in Wales

19 All of the neighbours' comments in lines 67–73 seem designed to do all of the following EXCEPT

    A reassure the old man
    B show their care for him
    C play on his weaknesses
    D express their impatience
    E overcome his longing for death

20 Grandfather was 'like a prophet who has no doubt' (line 75) most probably because

    A the end of the world was near
    B his neighbours were deceiving him
    C he was about to die at any moment
    D the river and sky had a message
    E God was about to speak to him

Now go back and check your work

Development

Further reading
D. Thomas, *Portrait of the Artist as a Young Dog* and *Quite Early one Morning*. Both of these books reveal the author's humour and close observation of people and their behaviour.

Listening
Listen to the radio play *Under Milk Wood* by Dylan Thomas. It is readily available as a gramophone record (Argo Mono ASW 501–2) and your local library would undoubtedly help you to obtain it. You will be fascinated by Dylan Thomas's portraits in sound of people he knew as a young man in 'a small town, starless and bible-black, the cobble-streets silent and the hunched courters'-and-rabbits' wood limping invisible down to the sloeblack, slow, black, crowblack, fishingboat-bobbing sea.'

Discussion
What is the role of old people in today's modern society? What can they contribute? What can we offer them? What are our responsibilities?
Discuss, perhaps with the help of one or two elderly visitors, some of the difficulties that young and old people have in adjusting to the others' views. Where do the differences really lie?

Essays
A terrible nightmare.
Dreams.
The secret of eternal youth.
Euthanasia.

Activities
Make a list of some interesting characteristics of an old person you know well. Try to find (or invent) words to describe the face, the walk, the stance of the person you choose. Think about some of the things he or she likes to do, his or her habits and mannerisms. You might like to add, too, some descriptive phrases that capture the mood of the house or flat he or she lives in. Then write your account in about 500 words.
Arrange a visit with some of your friends to an old man or woman living near you. Old people are often lonely and enjoy a visit from young people who are prepared to *listen* to them. (Arrangements would be best made by *one* of the class calling to start with; usually two, or at most three, are enough for an old person to cope with on any one visit.)

At twenty minutes past seven on Christmas Eve 1931 an army of insects began
to invade the bar of the Grand Hotel, Rangoon. They were pencil-shaped
creatures about four inches long and equipped with four distinct ways of
moving about. They could fly, weakly and sickeningly on long, floppy wings;
5   they could crawl on legs; they could wriggle on their stomachs; and most
startling of all, they could leap like rockets from end to end of the bar. By
half-past seven it was occupied territory. Men sat sweating in their shirt-
sleeves, with one hand covering up their drinks and the other flapping in front
of their faces.
10   The Mate of the paddle-steamer *Essex*, an aggressive young man from
Belfast, said to me: 'Let's get out of this. It's better on the boat.'
Forty years ago, for better or worse, I had adopted a hippy-like stance
towards life, well ahead of my time. At twenty what I liked best was to drift
about the world, cramming myself with as many of its strange flavours and
15   sensations as could be packed into each twenty-four hours. I had no other
ambitions, and South-East Asia in those days was exactly suited to my needs.
Conversation there had an agreeable dottiness; the people had more charm
than any others on earth. The girls were gorgeous, the sun was hot, travel was
easy, cheap, and primitive. Vietnam was still French Indo-China, famed for
20   an exciting night-life in Saigon. Thailand was Siam then, all temples and
dancing girls. And the Burmese were temporarily British—though it didn't
suit their temperament—and owned an enchanting river, the Irrawaddy. I'd
met the Mate of the *Essex* over a casual drink in the bar, and he had persuaded
me in no time that the best place for Christmas in Burma was on a paddle
25   steamer on the Irrawaddy. So we returned to our boat and beds.
The *Essex* lay tied to a jetty about five miles out of Rangoon. It was a big
boat, very broad, a three-decker with two enormous paddle-wheels. There was
a minute bridge, which included the Captain's cabin, and on the top deck
another six first-class cabins, one of them the Mate's, and a dining-room
30   which could comfortably seat eight or nine people. On the middle deck were
eight tiny second-class cabins, one of them belonging to the supercargo—a
Burmese who combined the jobs of tallyman and purser, counted the cargo,
received the fares, allotted the cabins, kept the cabin keys, superintended the
stowage, bullied the porters, and kept up a running battle with the Goanese
35   cook, who also lived in the second-class deck. The bowels of the ship were
entirely given over to McKay, the Chief Engineer, a great hairy Scot, and to

8

his mighty engines, and to his Anglo-Indian bosun and his Tamil stoker. Here they lived a separate life, supported almost entirely on whisky.

I'd had a row with the Mate about my clothes. I'd adopted the *lungje*, a very 40 simple cylinder of cotton cloth, fixed round the waist the way you fix a bath towel—by tucking it in. It was a perfect dress for the climate, but the Mate wouldn't have it. 'For God's sake don't let the old man see you. He has great ideas about the decadence of the white man and the spirit of the Empire.' So I arrived on board in a sahib's cotton suit with tie, a monstrous piece 45 of self-inflicted torture in a tropical country.

Christmas Day began at six o'clock in the morning when a Burmese steward woke me up. He was carrying a large tray on which were twenty tumblers half-filled with spirit. Gin, rum, brandy, whisky, both Irish and Scotch. There was a small carafe of water for the weaker brethren. I chose gin and went back 50 to sleep. At seven o'clock the steward brought another dose—and that's how Christmas Day wore on.

We clanked and chugged up river: twice in the morning we called at riverside villages, reflected golden in the water, to take on cargo—groundnuts. The sun shone, illuminating the golden-skinned Burmese in their golden villages, 55 where the white pagodas glittered with real gold on their spires. Every jetty was a riot of children in glorious colours, impertinent, wise-cracking, utterly unafraid children, children who had never been rebuked—or, according to the Mate, utterly spoiled children. The river was low, motor-oil green, smelt of marigolds. Dark jungle defined its banks, sometimes nearly a mile apart. We 60 had a man at the stern swinging the lead but nevertheless we touched sandbanks three times. Guinea-fowl and plum-pudding arrived at one o'clock. I wish I could say we were sober, but only the Captain passed that stern test. The Goanese cook caught three tremendous fish, each a yard long, on lines draped through the porthole of the galley. Extraordinary birds in gold and green and 65 vermilion settled on deck for a moment and took off again. 'Look at that bird,' the Captain said. 'What extravagance! Why does it have to be gold and green and black with yellow piping? How I long to see an English thrush again!'

At seven o'clock we hit a sandbank and the whole river suddenly began to seethe and wrinkle like milk at the boil. From the depths of the water rose 70 millions of hideous grey larvae, split along their backs, and ejected a sort of thing like a long furry bumble bee, only dark yellow. From these arose a frightful smell: not a healthy stink like rotten eggs, but an evil, thin, squalid, smell. 'Oh God,' said the Mate, 'they choose their hour! It's the night of the stink bugs!' And at that a great cloud of filthy things closed in on the boat. 75 Within ten minutes the deck was three inches thick in them—you slid about as if on snow. Every rope and stanchion wore a fur coat, every light was obscured as if by a swarm of bees or a bunch of grapes. Then as the sun set, a rifle cracked on the shore and a bullet went smack into one of the teak logs on the rail. The Mate was galvanised. He shouted, 'Unlock the rifles and 80 distribute them to the officers and first-class passengers.' More shots came.

continue overleaf

9

A cry went up, 'Sir, the Bo's gone.' And so it proved. The supercargo had gone too, and so had his pass-keys to the first-class cabins. The rope by which they had descended into the water hung from the side of the boat. An immense silver moon came up. Silence descended on the *Essex*, broken by the
85 Captain: 'Mister, get them started on the bugs. Shovels first, then brooms. And Steward, pass the drinks tray round, will you? What are you thinking about?'

René Cutforth, 'The Night of the Stink Bugs',
The Listener

1 The pencil-shaped creatures (lines 2–3) seemed able to do all of the following EXCEPT

- **A** fly nimbly about
- **B** creep along the floor
- **C** move on their bellies
- **D** jump long distances
- **E** penetrate indoors

2 The phrase 'occupied territory' (line 7) suggests that the

- **A** Japanese had arrived at the hotel
- **B** bar was busy and full of guests
- **C** navy had taken over full control
- **D** weather was so hot it was oppressive
- **E** insects were everywhere in the room

3 'Hippy-like' (line 12) in its context suggests mainly that the author

- **A** loved his fellow men
- **B** lived on drugs
- **C** preferred to roam about
- **D** wore his hair very long
- **E** had no money of his own

4 René Cutforth considers that being British did not suit the Burmese (lines 21–2) because they were essentially

- **A** uninterested in natural beauty
- **B** over-anxious to please
- **C** different in personality
- **D** unreliable in emergencies
- **E** easily roused to anger

10

5 The crew of the *Essex* had amongst its crew representatives of all the following nationalities EXCEPT

   A   Scots
   B   Vietnamese
   C   Burmese
   D   Goanese
   E   Irish

6 A 'supercargo' (line 31) seems to be the member of the crew responsible for the

   A   navigation of the vessel
   B   freight and passengers
   C   comfort of the crew
   D   engines and machinery
   E   galleys and dining-rooms

7 As a person the Captain was clearly a man of

   A   inflexible attitudes
   B   decadent morals
   C   hesitant behaviour
   D   racial feelings
   E   drunken habits

8 The Mate disapproved of the author's wearing a Burmese *lungje* because he knew that

   A   the Burmese would be offended by it
   B   it would suggest imperialism to the natives
   C   the Captain would be very angry
   D   it was inappropriate dress for the tropics
   E   the garment was not practical on board ship

9 Which of the following were literally golden?

   A   The reflections of the villages
   B   The villages themselves
   C   The skins of the Burmese
   D   The spires of the pagodas
   E   The birds of the jungle

continue overleaf

10 The man at the stern 'swinging the lead' (line 60) was

A trying to catch fish
B avoiding doing his work
C looking out for obstacles ahead
D seeing how deep the river was
E measuring the distance travelled

11 The 'stern test' (line 62) passed by the Captain was his success in

A giving orders clearly
B keeping sober
C providing a meal
D being punctual
E avoiding the sandbanks

12 A 'galley' (line 64) on board ship is the

A bridge
B mess-room
C kitchen
D rest-room
E washroom

13 The Captain's remark 'What extravagance!' (line 66) as he looked at the birds on the deck suggests that he

A was really very puritanical in all his views
B hated everything about the Far East
C was very unobservant about nature
D preferred the colours of garden birds
E was very patriotic in everything

14 The river 'suddenly began to seethe and wrinkle like milk at the boil' (lines 68-9) because

A the screws of the boat were lifting out of the water
B yellow insects were skimming low over the surface
C the boat was foundering on the river's muddy bottom
D the mud from the sandbank was being churned up
E insect larvae had started to rise to the surface

15 The smell is described as 'squalid' (line 72) because it was

A weak
B pungent
C choking
D overwhelming
E foul

16 The Mate's cry, 'It's the night of the stink bugs!' (lines 73–4) most probably suggests that the occurrence was

- A a recurring and well-known event
- B part of a deliberate attack on them
- C a regular incident on Christmas Day
- D something the natives laughed about
- E a situation that could have fatal results

17 'As if on snow' (line 76) is an unusual comparison to make for all of the following reasons EXCEPT that snow is

- A always freezing cold
- B not often seen in those parts
- C white and the bugs are yellow
- D very slippery underfoot
- E free from all smell

18 Which of the following is nearest in meaning to 'galvanised' as it is used in line 79?

- A Shocked into action
- B Baffled and bemused
- C Excited and bright
- D Stunned into silence
- E Encouraged by authority

19 The 'Bo' (line 81) most likely refers to the

- A nickname by which the supercargo was known
- B ship's Mate who came from Belfast
- C main lifeboat slung alongside
- D Anglo-Indian who helped Mr McKay
- E overhead radio-communication line

20 The Captain's order to 'pass the drinks tray round' (line 86) suggests that he

- A had now decided to become drunk
- B knew their position was quite hopeless
- C realised the men needed it to face their task
- D saw that they now had plenty of drink to use up
- E had seen the longing look in the author's eye

Now go back and check your work

Development

Further reading
Joseph Conrad's *Lord Jim*. This is an evocative story of the sea and sailors. In fact, Conrad's stories are often powerful in creating an atmosphere of the East and they explore man's own weaknesses in the face of unknown powers. The author had travelled far as a sailor in the Indian Ocean and near the Malay Peninsula.

Discussion
What justification is there today for adopting a 'hippy' way of life?

Written work
What do you think would be an appropriate way for you to extend your knowledge of the world and its peoples when you are about twenty?
Write an imaginative description of a journey up a river. (Attempt, as one of your main aims, to create atmosphere and tension.)

Projects
The development of the British Empire in the Far East.
The struggle for independence of India, Pakistan or Bangladesh.
The Burma Campaign of the 1939–45 War.

No one can really say when San Francisco's time will run out, in a repetition
of the terrible earthquake of 1906. Some day the western suburbs will slide
horizontally northwestwards past the city centre, again in a mighty jerk, like
the sudden release of a spring. The longer it is delayed, the worse it will be—
5 unless a small band of American specialists fulfil their present hopes and
tame the Californian earthquakes in time to save San Francisco. It is a worth-
while ambition, because pessimists say there could be 50,000 dead. Their
hopes are the outcome of an investigation that began in a bizarre way, with
the US Army trying to rid itself of poisonous chemicals. That was early in
10 1963, at the Rocky Mountain Arsenal, in Colorado, but close to the city of
Denver. Six weeks after the Army began pumping contaminated water down
a well two miles deep, Denver experienced its first earthquake in eighty years.
 Several years were to pass before the Army unwillingly admitted a possible
connection between its pumping activities and the long series of minor earth-
15 quakes that followed. But the pressure of the water had reactivated an old
fault deep underground, causing rocks to crack and allowing them to shift
more easily.
 So, the pressure of water in the rocks of a fault helps to determine whether
or not the fault will move. But any thought of applying this knowledge use-
20 fully relies upon the new grasp of the fundamental processes that cause earthquakes. During the past five years, there has been a revolution in the earth
sciences, involving a theory called 'plate tectonics' which states that the outer-
most shell of the earth, the top forty miles or so, is broken up into a number of
plates. There are six large ones—the American, Eurasian, African, Indian,
25 Pacific and Antarctic plates. These plates are jostling one another by moving
about in different directions, but the plates themselves are rigid. Nearly all
earthquakes originate at the margins of plates.
 The earthquakes of California mark a boundary between plates. At the
notorious San Andreas fault, which cuts across the State from the Gulf of
30 California to San Francisco, the Pacific plate and the American plate are in
relative movement. But they are scarcely moving apart or converging; instead
they are sidling past one another along what has come to be called a 'transform
fault'. The coastal strip of California is riding northwest on the Pacific plate
past the rest of the continent, at an average speed of twenty feet per century.
35 In about eight million years, Los Angeles will be alongside San Francisco.
continue overleaf

A question of life or death for people living on a plate boundary is whether it moves frequently, in a whole lot of minor earthquakes, or whether it sticks for long periods and then jerks, causing a major disaster. The answer can vary from place to place on the same plate boundary. In some parts of California the two sides of the fault are shuffling past one another with very little disturbance while at San Francisco the rocks are temporarily locked, allowing strain to accumulate in an ominous fashion. The sudden release of pent-up energy at the fault is like an explosion deep in the earth. The energy of the San Francisco earthquake of 1906, by no means the world's worst of this century, was equivalent to the explosion of a 100-megaton bomb.

The earthquake controllers cannot, like latter-day Canutes, command the plates to halt. What they would like to do is to smooth the movements at a plate boundary—in other words, to substitute a large number of minor earthquakes for the rare one of great violence. The results of experiments show, in principle, how it could be done. Pumping water into the deep-lying rocks of a fault can cause earthquakes; by that means a fault can be kept moving and not allowed to become locked and over-strained.

The catch is, of course, that parts of the San Andreas fault are already greatly strained. Simply to pump water into the fault near San Francisco could well trigger the very disaster that everyone fears. For this reason, the earthquake controllers' scheme is more subtle. The force of an earthquake depends on how great a portion of a fault moves at one time, so they would exploit the discovery that drying-out a fault makes it less likely to move. They would confine any man-made earthquake to a pre-selected length of the fault, supposedly too short to allow a major earthquake.

In practice this would mean boring a group of three holes, spaced at intervals of about 500 yards along the fault. From the outlying holes, natural water would be pumped out of the ground, to lock the fault at those two points; then, water pumped into the middle hole would cause minor earthquakes, to take the strain out of the rocks. Finally, pumping the water back out of the middle would leave the sector secure—at least for the time being. 'Debugging' the San Andreas fault system would require altogether about 500 permanent bore-holes, each going about three miles deep and costing about a million dollars. Yet $500 million is small compared with the estimated material damage of a major earthquake, in San Francisco alone.

N. Calder, 'Earthquakes', *Observer Magazine*

1 The 1906 San Francisco earthquake was caused by

    A   the sideways movements of land surfaces
    B   a sudden upsurge of hidden springs
    C   a fault having drill-holes bored along it
    D   a megaton bomb being exploded underground
    E   the pressure of water collecting in underground lakes

2 According to the author, the next earthquake in San Francisco will be all the following EXCEPT

- **A** worse as it is delayed
- **B** unexpected
- **C** impossible to predict accurately
- **D** sudden
- **E** costly in lives and money

3 The earthquakes in Denver in 1963 were caused by

- **A** chemicals eating away the underground rocks
- **B** constant vibration of the pumps
- **C** explosions destroying the underground rocks
- **D** gradual collapse of the deep well's sides
- **E** water pressure weakening the rock structure

4 The American army appears to have admitted the connection between its pumping activities and the 1963 earthquakes in Denver

- **A** generously and readily
- **B** with astonishment
- **C** slowly and reluctantly
- **D** with anger
- **E** unambiguously and promptly

5 The method proposed for saving San Francisco from future earthquakes is based on the theory that the

- **A** earthquakes at a fault occur with increasing violence
- **B** energy of earthquakes is provided by underground explosions
- **C** plate on which the coastal strip of California is riding can be halted
- **D** water pressure in rocks is a factor in a fault's movements
- **E** pumping-out of water from rocks will eventually cause an earthquake

6 'Plate tectonics' (line 22) is basically a theory that the earth's crust is

- **A** harder in some places than others
- **B** broken into vast moving pieces
- **C** thicker at the edges and shallower in the centre
- **D** divided into equal sized portions
- **E** round in shape and easily fractured

continue overleaf

7 The six large 'plates' of the Earth's crust are all said to be

1. eight million years old
2. moving northwards
3. inflexible in their structure
4. moving in different directions
5. forty miles or so thick

A   1, 2 and 3 only
B   1, 4 and 5 only
C   2, 3 and 4 only
D   2, 4 and 5 only
E   3, 4 and 5 only

8 According to the 'plate tectonics' theory most major earthquakes occur when

A   underground springs are compressed
B   the crust is less than forty miles thick
C   deep holes have been drilled in a series
D   the edges of plates stick together and build up strain
E   rocks have become fused together by heat

9 One place where the Earth's 'plates' are said to be in relative movement is

A   Denver
B   the Rocky Mountains
C   Los Angeles
D   the San Andreas fault
E   Colorado

10 At San Francisco the Pacific and American 'plates' at the moment are

A   moving easily
B   unlikely to move much
C   moving slowly
D   not moving at all
E   moving in jerks

11 According to the explanation of the 'plate tectonics' theory the Earth's major plates can do all of the following EXCEPT

A   rub past one another
B   move together
C   slide under one another
D   move apart
E   keep in line with one another

18

12 Which of the following is nearest in meaning to 'pent-up' as it is used in line 42?

A Imprisoned
B Massive
C Controlled
D Destructive
E Underground

13 Which of the following is nearest in meaning to 'latter-day' as it is used in line 46?

A Future
B Modern
C Recent
D Old
E Dead

14 At San Francisco two of the Earth's 'plates' are likely to move

A violently together and upwards
B gradually apart
C steadily northwestwards
D slowly downwards
E suddenly past each other

15 The author suggests that the main aim of scientists dealing with earthquakes at San Francisco is to

A extract the corrosive chemicals from beneath the city
B lock the rock-fault underground to prevent its movement
C build shock-proof buildings and earthquake centres
D compare scientifically the next earthquake due with that of 1906
E replace a possible large future earthquake with many small ones

16 Pumping water into the whole fault beneath San Francisco could well result in

A a violent earthquake
B temporary safety
C many small earthquakes
D permanent stability
E a gentle subsidence

17 Locking a fault (line 63) is achieved by

A drilling holes into it
B pumping away all the water there
C neutralising it with chemicals
D exploding bombs in it
E digging it out with machinery

continue overleaf

18 The scheme for preventing a violent earthquake at San Francisco involves all the following EXCEPT

    A   drilling lines of holes in groups of three
    B   pumping water from two outlying holes
    C   filling in the two outlying holes
    D   pumping water into the centre hole
    E   pumping water out of the centre hole later

19 The results of an uncontrolled earthquake happening unexpectedly at San Francisco are forecast as

    1   more than fifty thousand dead
    2   the release of poisonous chemicals underground
    3   more than five hundred million dollars' worth of damage
    4   the release of enormous underground floods

    A   1 and 2 only
    B   1 and 3 only
    C   2 and 3 only
    D   2 and 4 only
    E   3 and 4 only

20 The author's main point appears to be that a future earthquake at San Francisco could be

    A   ignored for the present
    B   useful to science
    C   prevented by the right measures
    D   diverted into the Pacific
    E   exaggerated by writers

Now go back and check your work

Development

Discussion
What international organisations could be set up to help with natural disasters?

How can San Francisco prepare for a possible earthquake?
Why do people live in areas liable to be destroyed suddenly by nature?

Essays
Can the forces of the natural world be harnessed more effectively for man's good?
The river of fire.
Write the story of a rescue from a collapsing building, *either* as if you were the rescuer *or* as if you were the person being saved.

Projects
Earthquake areas of the world.
Great earthquakes of the past.
Local organisations that will deal with emergencies and disasters.

It was the Indians' uncompromising refusal to surrender their legal title to the Black Hills that brought Congress to enforce the 'purchase' of the tribes' lands. In 1872, the troops of Generals Custer and Reno bore down on the Sioux lodges on the Little Bighorn. The war chief who rallied the Sioux
5 Indians and turned back Reno's attack was a 36-year-old Hunkpapa named Gall.

Some years before, while the commissioners were attempting to persuade the Sioux to take up farming as a part of the treaty of 1868, Gall went to Fort Rice to speak for the Hunkpapas. 'We were born naked,' he said, 'and have
10 been taught to hunt and live on the game. You tell us that we must learn to farm, live in one house, and take on your ways. Suppose the people living beyond the great sea should come and tell you that you must stop farming and kill your cattle, and take your houses and lands, what would you do? Would you not fight them?'

15 In military terms, Gall turned Reno's flank and forced him into the woods. He then frightened Reno into making a hasty retreat which the Indians quickly turned into a rout. The result made it possible for Gall to divert hundreds of warriors for a frontal attack against Custer's 260 men at Little Bighorn, while Crazy Horse struck the flanks and rear. According to Red
20 Horse, toward the end of fighting with Custer, 'these soldiers became foolish, many throwing away their guns and raising their hands, saying, "Sioux, pity us; take us prisoners." The Sioux did not take a single soldier prisoner, but killed all of them.' When the white men in the East heard of the Long Hair's death and defeat at Little Bighorn they called it a massacre and went crazy
25 with anger.

On July 22, 1877, the Great Warrior Sherman received authority to assume military control of all reservations in the Sioux country and to treat the Indians there as prisoners of war. On August 15 the Great Council of the USA made a new law requiring the Indians to give up all rights to the Black
30 Hills. They did this without regard to the treaty of 1868, maintaining that the Indians had violated the treaty by going to war with the United States. This was difficult for the reservation Indians to understand, because they had not attacked United States soldiers first, nor had Sitting Bull's followers attacked them until Custer sent Reno charging through the Sioux villages.

35 The Great Father in Washington sent out a new commission in September to cajole and threaten the chiefs and secure their signatures to legal documents

22

transferring the Black Hills to white ownership. To break down their opposition, the commissioners dropped strong hints that unless they signed, the Great Council in its anger would cut off all rations immediately, would re-
40 move them to the Indian Territory in the south, and the Army would take all their guns and horses. There was no way out, and the land of the Black Hills, its spirits and its mysteries, its vast pine forests and its billion dollars in gold passed on for ever from the hands of the Indians into the domain of the United States.

45 After the 1877 surrender Sitting Bull, one of the great Sioux war leaders, spent some years in Canada with a band of his people, but nostalgia for their old lands drove them back to the reservations on the Black Hills. Sitting Bull lived peaceably, giving interviews to newspapers, touring in a Wild West show. But in 1890 a new religion, the 'Dance of the Ghosts', was brought to the
50 bitter and hopeless Indians. By mid-November Ghost Dancing was so prevalent on the Sioux reservations that almost all other activities came to a halt and no work was done on the little farms.

On November 20 the Indian Bureau in Washington ordered agents in the field to telegraph the names of all 'fomenters of disturbances' among the
55 Ghost Dancers. A list was transmitted to Bear Coat Miles's Army headquarters in Chicago. Miles saw Sitting Bull's name on it and immediately assumed that he was to blame for all the disturbances. On December 15, 1890, forty-three Indian police surrounded Sitting Bull's log-cabin, and he was arrested by Lieutenant Bull Head, the Indian policeman in charge of the party.

60 When Bull Head emerged from the cabin with Sitting Bull he found a crowd of Ghost Dancers gathering outside. But Sitting Bull held back, making it necessary for Bull Head and Sergeant Red Tomahawk to force him toward his horse. At this moment, Catch-the-Bear threw off his blanket and brought up a rifle. He fired at Bull Head, wounding him in the side. Almost simul-
65 taneously, Red Tomahawk shot Sitting Bull through the head and killed him. During the firing, the old show-horse that Buffalo Bill had presented to Sitting Bull began to go through his tricks. He sat upright, raised one hoof, and it seemed to those who watched that he was performing the Dance of the Ghosts.

D. Brown, 'Revenge at Wounded Knee',
The Sunday Times Magazine

1 The Hunkpapas appear to have been

    A   the main possessors of Black Hills land
    B   a sub-tribe of the Sioux
    C   the Indians who lived and worked naked
    D   a tribe at war with the Sioux
    E   the chief practisers of ghost dancing

continue overleaf

2 Which of the following is nearest in meaning to 'uncompromising' as it is used in line 1 ?

    A Yielding
    B Reliable
    C Rigid
    D Understanding
    E Inclusive

3 All the following were Sioux Indians EXCEPT

    A Gall
    B Crazy Horse
    C Long Hair
    D Sitting Bull
    E Catch-the-Bear

4 The treaty of 1868 appears to have

    A enforced the selling of Sioux land where necessary
    B made a joint American-Sioux defence pact against foreign invasion
    C given every member of the Sioux a legal title to a farm
    D guaranteed parts of the Black Hills as Sioux reservations
    E forbidden the Sioux to possess either horses or guns

5 The commissioners dealing with the Sioux Indians before 1872 appear to have ad their headquarters in

    A Fort Rice
    B Canada
    C Washington
    D Little Bighorn
    E Chicago

6 The aims of the commissioners appear to have been to persuade the Sioux to

    1 wear clothes
    2 become farmers
    3 have a settled abode
    4 fight for their rights
    5 adopt American customs

    A 1, 2 and 4 only
    B 1, 2 and 5 only
    C 1, 3 and 4 only
    D 2, 3 and 5 only
    E 3, 4 and 5 only

7 'Turned Reno's flank' (line 15) is best explained as

   A wounded Reno in the side while he was off guard
   B passed round Reno's troops and attacked them from the side
   C caused Reno's troops to lose their nerve and break in disorder
   D compelled Reno to go searching for him in the woods
   E made Reno over-confident and changed his attitude

8 At Little Bighorn Custer's soldiers were all of the following EXCEPT

   A surrounded
   B attacked by Gall's braves
   C unyielding
   D attacked by Crazy Horse's braves
   E annihilated

9 'They called it a massacre' (line 24) implies that

   A the Little Bighorn defeat had destroyed the American army
   B women, children, and non-combatants had been killed
   C the Americans were trying to play down their defeat
   D all Custer's troops without exception were annihilated
   E the Americans always treated the Indians honourably

10 The white men 'went crazy with anger' (lines 24–5) with all of the following results EXCEPT that the Sioux

   A were killed in large numbers as a reprisal
   B reservations were placed under the Army's authority
   C Indians already on reservations were made prisoners of war
   D ownership of the Black Hills was to be brought to an end
   E were sent another commission to investigate their claims

11 After Little Bighorn the Sioux on the reservations were puzzled by the American accusation that they had violated the 1868 treaty because the Sioux

   A had approved all its terms
   B were unwilling to face the truth
   C could not understand the legal language
   D had had no experience of American treachery
   E were not the first aggressors

12 The Sioux's opposition to giving up the Black Hills was broken down by threats that they would lose all of the following EXCEPT their

   A reservations
   B rations
   C firearms
   D horses
   E identity

continue overleaf

13 The Americans wanted to acquire the Black Hills mainly for their

    A scenic beauty
    B political importance
    C potential wealth
    D romantic mystery
    E military value

14 Sitting Bull went to Canada (lines 45–6) presumably to

    A stir up hate towards the Americans
    B avoid arrest by the army
    C start a Wild West show
    D avoid the disgrace of defeat
    E learn Ghost Dancing

15 Between 1877 and his death in 1890 Sitting Bull spent at one period or another a substantial time in all of the following EXCEPT

    A living in exile
    B working in show business
    C fighting other Indians
    D associating with Ghost Dancers
    E talking to journalists

16 The main reason for Sitting Bull's return to the Black Hills was

    A hardship from poverty
    B wander-lust
    C desire for fame
    D home-sickness
    E hostility from Canadians

17 In order to control the Indians, by 1890 the American government had all of the following EXCEPT

    A an Indian Bureau in Washington
    B representatives working amongst the Indians
    C an army headquarters established in Chicago
    D Indian policemen to keep the peace
    E the active support of Sitting Bull

18 Catch-the-Bear can most obviously be identified as

    A an army officer
    B a Ghost Dancer
    C an Indian policeman
    D a hired assassin
    E an American agent

26

19 For those involved in the incident the behaviour of Sitting Bull's horse during the killing of his master can best be described as

A ironic
B uninteresting
C irrelevant
D amusing
E predictable

20 All the following Americans are given their Indian titles in the passage EXCEPT

A General Custer
B General Sherman
C The President
D General Miles
E General Reno

Now go back and check your work

Development

Further reading
Jack Schaefer, *Shane* and *The Pioneers*. The second of these books is a collection of short stories about the conquest of the West. Zane Grey, *Wildfire* (a story of a man's attempt to catch a wild stallion).

Discussion
Why is it more popular today than in previous times to sympathise with the Indians?
What can the Americans (or the British) do to ease their racial tensions?
Is violence ever justifiable?
Can warfare ever have rules? If so, are there any new ones to add?

Essays
Lost in the wilderness.
The Last Stand.
Problems of minority races in the world today.
What is there still to admire in primitive cultures?
Write an essay as if you were *either* Crazy Horse *or* Custer explaining why Little Bighorn occurred.

Projects

The Red Indian tribes of North America—their similarities and differences.
The customs and beliefs of North American Indians.
Red Indian art.
The causes and events of the American conquest of the West.
The American army in the nineteenth century.

Activities

During the next month arrange to watch four TV westerns in which either Indians or the American armed forces of the period have a major part. Divide the study class into four groups, each of which will observe and report on *one* of the following aspects:

(a) The role of the individual Indian or soldier.
(b) The underlying values implicit in the behaviour of either Indians or soldiers.
(c) Dramatic features in the presentation of Indians or soldiers.
(d) Degrees of bias in the presentation of Indians and soldiers.

The four groups should then report to the class as a whole what they have noticed.

ALAN BARKER is a public school headmaster. Unlike most headmasters, he is active politically. He is a Tory Alderman of Cambridgeshire County. His school is called The Leys and all the boys there are fee-paying.

Mr Barker thinks the middle-class intelligentsia gets itself unduly worked
5 up over issues like corporal punishment. He doesn't think it very important. 'No master can beat a boy without asking me first. None has asked me in two years. I haven't beaten anybody for about six months, as far as I know.' He tells me about some fourteen-year-old boys who broke a rule about climbing on a construction company's fence. 'Instead of giving them a great harangue,
10 I spanked them. We had no more trouble. I would never use the cane on a boy much older than fourteen or fifteen. I don't think of it as being an ultimate deterrent. I use it in the same way I did with Bumble as a puppy.' Bumble is a boxer, a constant presence in the Barker household.

Mr Barker has total confidence in the police. On the two occasions when
15 drug-taking was discovered at The Leys, he quickly called in the police. Most parents would not turn in their own children. As the headmaster is *in loco parentis*, does he not at least hesitate before calling in the police? 'No. I think you are obliged to bring the police in. Even if you weren't, I think you should do so. Drugs can be surrounded with deceit and lies and the underground and
20 so on. I would think it automatic to bring the police in—both because of the law and because they can give practical help.' The police are primarily concerned to find the source of supply, he says.

'I think the great heresy of the last twenty-five years is the view that the world will be made better if only people will share their advantages. I think
25 the world can only be redeemed by the few who have advantages. You must think realistically about this. It would be awfully nice to feel that one is doing a job for the underprivileged, but one can't do both. You are either running a fee-paying school or a State boarding school. There is no compromise solution.'

30 If Mr Barker feels impatience with his colleagues who nurse a social conscience, he feels only contempt for the middle-class intelligentsia who want public schools abolished simply so that they don't have to make the choice of whether to send their children there or whether to practise the equality they preach. 'Until people who feel we ought to get rid of the public schools stop

continue overleaf

35 sending their own children to them, you really cannot expect people who are
not left-wing to behave differently.'

Doctor ROYSTON LAMBERT is the headmaster of Dartington Hall. The boys
and girls at his school call him Roy. Dartington Hall is a famous progressive
school. Boys and girls there can do what they like.
40   'I've come to this school with a programme,' he says. 'It used to be cosy and
intimate and inward-looking, catering only for the trendy few who thought
they were radical because of trivial things like mixed nude bathing.' It'll
never be like that again. 'The Dartington endowment was being used to keep
fees at a low level, however rich parents were. I've withdrawn this endowment
45 from well-off parents and used it for the Yorkshire scheme, of giving 6th
form education to working-class Yorkshire children—in my view for the
benefit of everybody.'
   He has the entire staff's support in his attitude towards things like violence
and drugs. The question of caning, of course, would never arise at a school like
50 this. 'Violence has no justification except the emotional release for the person
doing it,' says Dr Lambert. We should be concerned for the recipients—not
with gratifying our less good impulses. 'I don't know of a case where any
staff here has hit anyone. If it happened, it would be an understandable act:
that's life. But it's not a good thing.'
55   If a child is known to be smoking pot—and at Dartington Hall the children
would usually discuss it with the staff—the matter is not reported to the
police. 'We talk it over with the children. Pot is socially withdrawing: although
they sit together with others when they're smoking, it's not true communica-
tion. And they become unaware of their own situation. Every effort is made
60 to get the child off pot. Usually we succeed. We have better relations with the
police than for many years. They give talks here. I've worked with them to
keep drug pedlars from coming on to the estate. But I wouldn't report a child.
Children on pot are usually people with problems. The trauma of a police
investigation would only upset them more and make matters worse. How can
65 you look someone in the face if you say you want to help him and you go to
the police to produce this help? I don't believe in money buying you exemp-
tion from anything. But I think it is our responsibility to deal with the child
and give him sympathy and support. If our kids fall foul of the law and the
police discover it, OK. Otherwise we must sort it out ourselves.'
70   Among the untrendy fee-paying parents whom Dr Lambert has attracted
to Dartington is a chief constable.

Susan Barnes, 'Two Thoughts of School',
The Sunday Times Magazine

1 Alan Barker is said to be different from most headmasters because he

    A is confident about the police's ability
    B thinks like a Conservative
    C is willing to use corporal punishment
    D takes part actively in politics
    E is impatient with his colleagues

2 According to the passage, all the following seem true of The Leys School EXCEPT that it

    A has an alderman as its headmaster
    B takes in only fee-paying pupils
    C has never had any drug problems
    D accepts only boys as its pupils
    E has the status of a public school

3 Mr Barker does not appear to agree with middle-class people who

    1 send their children to state schools
    2 become excited about corporal punishment
    3 want public schools abolished to spare their consciences
    4 prefer schools to be run by left-wing headmasters
    5 think the police should be called in on all drug cases

    A 1 and 4 only
    B 1 and 5 only
    C 2 and 3 only
    D 2 and 4 only
    E 3 and 5 only

4 Corporal punishment at The Leys is given

    1 only with the headmaster's consent
    2 only whenever a member of the staff thinks it necessary
    3 only if the offender is under fifteen
    4 in all cases of drug offences

    A 1 and 2 only
    B 1 and 3 only
    C 2 and 3 only
    D 2 and 4 only
    E 3 and 4 only

continue overleaf

5 Which of the following is nearest in meaning to 'harangue' as it is used in line 9?

    A Loud speech
    B Imposition
    C Public humiliation
    D Beating
    E Lengthy essay

6 It is implied that Mr Barker punishes young boys as he did Bumble, the puppy, 'in the same way' (line 12) in order to show them

    A he is their lord and master
    B they must learn to obey the rules
    C he really loves them quite a lot
    D they are behaving in a childish way
    E he really wants to forget the offence

7 Mr Barker is said to differ in attitude from most of his pupils' parents by

    A using occasional corporal punishment
    B believing in the public school system
    C continuing to respect the law
    D having firm political beliefs
    E being willing to report his charges to the police

8 Mr Barker calls in the police when drug-taking is discovered in his school because they

    1 will deal ruthlessly with culprits
    2 can give help in a real way
    3 have to be notified by law
    4 always find the source of the drugs

    A 1 and 2 only
    B 1 and 3 only
    C 2 and 3 only
    D 2 and 4 only
    E 3 and 4 only

9 In drug offences the main interest of the police is to

    A arrest the worst offenders
    B find where the drugs are hidden
    C keep the matter secret
    D learn where the drugs are coming from
    E give helpful advice

10 Mr Barker, it is argued, believes that the world can be saved only by the

A middle-class intelligentsia
B staffs of public schools
C minority in privileged positions
D population's confidence in the police
E people of left-wing opinions

11 Mr Barker appears to think that drug-taking also involves

1 lying
2 people desiring an alternative society
3 deception
4 people who will blackmail his pupils
5 illness

A 1, 2 and 3 only
B 1, 4 and 5 only
C 2, 3 and 4 only
D 2, 4 and 5 only
E 3, 4 and 5 only

12 Two beliefs of Mr Barker appear to be that

1 all headmasters should lead some kind of political life
2 people who dislike public schools should not send their children there
3 corporal punishment is the best way to discipline all schoolboys
4 his school cannot combine private and state-aided pupils

A 1 and 2 only
B 1 and 3 only
C 2 and 3 only
D 2 and 4 only
E 3 and 4 only

13 According to the passage, all the pupils at Dartington Hall appear to be

1 on familiar terms with the headmaster
2 able to do what they like
3 drawn from the same social class
4 helped with the payment of their fees
5 free from official corporal punishment

A 1, 2 and 3 only
B 1, 2 and 5 only
C 2, 3 and 4 only
D 2, 4 and 5 only
E 3, 4 and 5 only

continue overleaf

14 Under Dr Lambert, Dartington Hall no longer seems to

1 concern itself only with the trendy few
2 have an agreed approach to violence
3 be concerned with its own life
4 allow nude bathing
5 help every pupil with his fees

A 1, 2 and 3 only
B 1, 2 and 4 only
C 1, 3 and 5 only
D 2, 4 and 5 only
E 3, 4 and 5 only

15 According to the article, Dartington Hall differs from The Leys School in all of the following ways EXCEPT in

A giving free tuition to working-class children
B not having official corporal punishment
C being a mixed school
D not reporting drug offences to the police
E existing outside the state system

16 An 'endowment' (line 43) is best described as

A an income-tax return
B a set of regulations
C a security system
D a list of scholars
E a permanent income

17 Which of the following is nearest in meaning to 'trauma' as used in line 63?

A Detailed investigation
B Rigour
C Awkward questions
D Interference
E Emotional shock

18 It is suggested that Dr Lambert claims that he has his staff's total support in matters of

1 standards of dress
2 punishment
3 giving free education
4 drug-taking

34

A   1 and 2 only
B   1 and 3 only
C   2 and 3 only
D   2 and 4 only
E   3 and 4 only

19 The article probably quotes the example of a Dartington Hall parent being a chief constable to show that

A   socially responsible people accept Dr Lambert's methods
B   the police maintain close contact with the school
C   strict parents will have their ideas carried out there
D   trendy parents no longer send their children to the school
E   any problems about drugs in the school have now ended

20 Mr Barker and Dr Lambert have in common their

1   headships of public schools
2   political beliefs
3   methods of dealing with drug-takers
4   concern over pupils who take drugs
5   use of the police on occasion

A   1, 3 and 4 only
B   1, 4 and 5 only
C   2, 3 and 4 only
D   2, 4 and 5 only
E   3, 4 and 5 only

Now go back and check your work

Development

Discussion
How can young people be guided away from drugs?

Essays
'If I were a headmaster . . .' How would you organise a school to give the children the best chances of learning and the greatest happiness during the day?

A terrible interview and its consequences (or causes).

'Schooldays are the happiest days of your life.' What arguments can be put forward to support this statement or to refute it?

Suggest some solutions to the world's (or this country's) problem of drug-taking.

How would you raise children of your own to ensure their health, wealth, and happiness?

Projects

The organisation of education in this country.

Class divisions in English society.

Secondary education in your area.

Discipline in schools.

Some schools found in literature.

Activities

Arrange a visit to (or from) a college of education in your area in order to discover how teachers are prepared for work in the schools. You may wish to write to a number of colleges throughout the country (their addresses are to be found in the A.T.C.D.E. *Handbook on Colleges of Education* in your reference library) in order to get copies of their prospectuses, from which you will be able to learn much about where they place their emphasis.

A Working Party

Three hours ago he blundered up the trench,
Sliding and poising, groping with his boots;
Sometimes he tripped and lurched against the walls
With hands that pawed the sodden bags of chalk.
5 He couldn't see the man who walked in front;
Only he heard the drum and rattle of feet
Stepping along barred trench boards, often splashing
Wretchedly where the sludge was ankle-deep.

Voices would grunt 'Keep to your right—make way!'
10 When squeezing past some men from the front-line:
White faces peered, puffing a point of red;
Candles and braziers glinted through the chinks
And curtain-flaps of dug-outs; then the gloom
Swallowed his sense of sight; he stooped and swore
15 Because a sagging wire had caught his neck.
A flare went up; the shining whiteness spread
And flickered upward, showing nimble rats
And mounds of glimmering sand-bags, bleached with rain;
Then the slow silver moment died in dark.
20 The wind came posting by with chilly gusts
And buffeting at corners, piping thin
And dreary through the crannies; rifle-shots
Would split and crack and sing along the night,
And shells came calmly through the drizzling air
25 To burst with hollow bang below the hill.
Three hours ago he stumbled up the trench;
Now he will never walk that road again:
He must be carried back, a jolting lump
Beyond all need of tenderness and care.

30 He was a young man with a meagre wife
And two small children in a Midland town;

continue overleaf

He showed their photographs to all his mates,
And they considered him a decent chap
Who did his work and hadn't much to say,
35 And always laughed at other people's jokes
Because he hadn't any of his own.

That night when he was busy at his job
Of piling bags along the parapet,
He thought how slow time went, stamping his feet
40 And blowing on his fingers, pinched with cold.
He thought of getting back by half-past twelve,
And tot of rum to send him warm to sleep
In draughty dug-out frowsty with the fumes
Of coke, and full of snoring weary men.

45 He pushed another bag along the top,
Craning his body outward; then a flare
Gave one white glimpse of No Man's Land and wire;
And as he dropped his head the instant split
His startled life with lead, and all went out.

Siegfried Sassoon

High Wood

Ladies and gentlemen, this is High Wood,
Called by the French, Bois des Fourneaux,
The famous spot which in Nineteen-Sixteen,
July, August and September was the scene
5 Of long and bitterly contested strife,
By reason of its high commanding site.
Observe the effect of shell-fire in the trees
Standing and fallen; here is wire; this trench
For months inhabited, twelve times changed hands,
10 (They soon fall in), used later as a grave.
It has been said on good authority
That in the fighting for this patch of wood
Were killed somewhere above eight thousand men,
Of whom the greater part were buried here,
15 This mound on which you stand being . . .

Madame, please,

You are requested kindly not to touch
Or take away the Company's property
As souvenirs; you'll find we have on sale
20 A large variety, all guaranteed.
As I was saying, all is as it was,

This is an unknown British officer,
The tunic having lately rotted off.
Please follow me—this way . . .
25   the *path*, sir, *please*,
The ground which was secured at great expense
The Company keeps absolutely untouched,
And in that dug-out (genuine) we provide
Refreshments at a reasonable rate.
30   You are requested not to leave about
Paper, or ginger-beer bottles, or orange-peel.
There are waste-paper baskets at the gate.

Philip Johnstone

A Working Party

1 All of the following words in the first stanza suggest that the man found the trench very wet EXCEPT

A   sliding (line 2)
B   sodden (line 4)
C   rattle (line 6)
D   splashing (line 7)
E   sludge (line 8)

2 Which of the following is most strongly suggested by the words of the first stanza?

A   Hope
B   Patriotism
C   Coldness
D   Uncertainty
E   Determination

3 On his way along the trench which of the following does the soldier see distinctly?

A   The men who grunt instructions at him
B   The facial features of the men from the front line
C   The burning glow of men's cigarettes
D   The interior of dug-outs through curtain flaps
E   The barbed wire which caught at his neck

continue overleaf

4 'A flare went up' (line 16) is an effective moment in the poem for all of the following reasons EXCEPT

    A   its whiteness spreading out contrasts with the previous darkness
    B   the soldier was able to find his bearings for the first time
    C   it highlights the abject squalor of life in the trenches
    D   the enemy's threatening presence and signs of war are obvious
    E   it is a symbolic sign of the peace to come eventually

5 Which of the following is nearest in meaning to 'posting' as it is used in line 20?

    A   Hurrying
    B   Howling
    C   Banging
    D   Eddying
    E   Dropping

6 'Split and crack and sing' (line 23) are probably meant to suggest the noise of

    1   a bullet striking an object
    2   the cry of a man being wounded
    3   a rifle being fired
    4   the ricocheting of a bullet
    5   a stone disintegrating on impact

    A   1, 2, and 3 only
    B   1, 3, and 4 only
    C   2, 3, and 4 only
    D   2, 4, and 5 only
    E   3, 4, and 5 only

7 Lines 26–9 do all of the following EXCEPT deliberately

    A   contrast the soldier's way along the trench and his return
    B   show how awkward and difficult the trench was to negotiate
    C   illustrate how long the soldier had remained in the trench
    D   imply that the soldier never had any feelings in the trench
    E   reveal that those wounded in the trench would be looked after

8 The third stanza (lines 30–6) reveals all the following about the soldier EXCEPT that he was

    A   without a sense of humour
    B   proud of his family
    C   still not very old
    D   considered a good fellow
    E   really rather quiet

9 The fourth stanza (lines 37–44) deliberately emphasises all the following EXCEPT the

- **A**   routine nature of a soldier's work
- **B**   boredom of trench warfare on quiet nights
- **C**   drunkenness of the ordinary soldier
- **D**   longing for comfort by soldiers out on duty
- **E**   tiredness produced by trench warfare

10 The last words of the poem, 'all went out' (line 49) means that the

- **A**   soldier had died
- **B**   flare had burnt out
- **C**   soldier had fallen asleep
- **D**   coke fires had died down
- **E**   night's work had ended

High Wood

11 Most probably the 'ladies and gentlemen' of line 1 are

- 1   the poem's readers
- 2   a theatre audience
- 3   English tourists
- 4   company representatives

- **A**   1 and 2 only
- **B**   1 and 3 only
- **C**   2 and 3 only
- **D**   2 and 4 only
- **E**   3 and 4 only

12 The attitude of the speaker towards the fighting at High Wood can best be described as

- 1   formal
- 2   enthusiastic
- 3   indifferent
- 4   amused

- **A**   1 and 2 only
- **B**   1 and 3 only
- **C**   2 and 3 only
- **D**   2 and 4 only
- **E**   3 and 4 only

continue overleaf

13 We are told that the reason why High Wood was the scene of fierce fighting was that

- **A** it overlooked the surrounding countryside
- **B** the soldiers there were selected for their courage
- **C** it was covered in trees useful for camouflage
- **D** the site was famous as a landmark
- **E** it provided a good trench network for defenders

14 The speaker's logical train of thought and matter-of-factness justify the reader in thinking that line 15 would have ended with the words

- **A** no-man's land
- **B** a gun emplacement
- **C** their high-command post
- **D** a dug-out
- **E** their grave

15 The phrase 'all guaranteed' (line 20) suggests that the souvenirs were

- **A** relics of the battle itself
- **B** articles sure not to break
- **C** goods that could be replaced
- **D** items approved by good taste
- **E** objects that really were definitely false

16 Line 25 with its words in italics suggests most strongly that

- **A** another guide was about to take over
- **B** a tourist was blocking the guide's way
- **C** the man in front should lead the party up
- **D** someone had strayed from the approved track
- **E** the guide was appealing for help to find the way

17 'The ground which was secured at great expense' (line 26) probably has the double meaning for the poet that

- 1 the Company spent a lot of money to restore it
- 2 fencing it off to make it safe caused a lot of trouble
- 3 many lives had been lost in capturing it in 1916
- 4 it had cost a lot to acquire it by purchase

- **A** 1 and 2 only
- **B** 1 and 3 only
- **C** 2 and 3 only
- **D** 2 and 4 only
- **E** 3 and 4 only

42

18 The futility and stupidity of war is made clear by all of the following EXCEPT that

    A   the dead had long since been buried and forgotten
    B   visitors showed little respect for those who had died
    C   the hill was won only to become a cheap tourist attraction
    D   men from both sides died and most were buried in the trench
    E   the Company preserved the site in its original condition

Both Poems

19 Both poems take as their main subject all of the following aspects of war EXCEPT its

    A   cost
    B   necessity
    C   uselessness
    D   agony
    E   inhumanity

20 Both poems are similar in all of the following respects EXCEPT that both

    A   evoke the pity that death in war arouses
    B   are concerned with the violence of war
    C   are written by the poets as spectators, not soldiers
    D   deal exclusively with an individual soldier
    E   take war in the trenches as their subject

Now go back and check your work

Development

Further reading
Robert Graves, *Goodbye to all that.* Siegfried Sassoon, *Memoirs of an Infantry Officer.* Both of these books contain graphic accounts of the tragedy of the First World War. The poems of Wilfred Owen, too, show poignantly the pity of war.

Discussion
Is there such a thing as a just war?
Pacifism and patriotism: are they in conflict?
What can we do to avoid further wars?
What part should the Church play in wars?

Essays
A day in the life of Tommy Atkins.
Man's inhumanity to man.
The greatest courage.

Projects
The Battle of Britain.
The Battles of the Somme.
The work of the Red Cross.

Activities
Play-reading. From your local library service obtain a set of R. C. Sheriff's *Journey's End*, a successful play which shows how men react to the stresses of war.

Call upon a war-pensioner who is lonely in your district or invite him to share in a discussion at school where his experiences would be invaluable. (You might ask your local branch of the British Legion to help you make contact with a suitable pensioner.)

Invite a priest or local clergyman to introduce a discussion about the moral questions which war poses for the modern teenager.

'I was brought *up* on Scott's Emulsion,' says the elderly chemist in his shop
in a shabby Islington street. Plump and pleasant and clean in his white coat,
he fondles the salmon-coloured pack with its homely drawing of an old
fisherman with a man-sized fish on his back.

5 'We still sell a lot of it. Funny thing, I used to hate it as a kid, but I love it
now—even the smell of it. It's got a terrible smell really: it's cod liver oil, you
know. But I *love* it now.' Associations with the safe and golden days of childhood, perhaps? He nods gently, warming to the idea. 'That's what it is.'

'A vitamin tonic food supplement,' it says on the Scott's pack. Particularly
10 useful for growing children, it's 'also beneficial for invalids, the aged and
others who need easily assimilated vitamin supplement.' It contains the world's
finest cod liver oil, it says, and is 'an invaluable aid to restore and maintain
health and strength.' It's very tempting: the claims are modest; the words are
buoyant and healthy.

15 New patent medicines are notoriously difficult to market. This Islington
chemist, as it happens, is a *placebo** in his own right and also conscientious.
With many elderly and poor people in the area, he cares about what they pay:
old customers will often allow themselves to be guided by him. Since prescription charges started, he says, purchases of patent medicines have greatly
20 increased. Every chemist he knows says the same.

Brand loyalty is strong. In the Piccadilly Circus branch of Boots, which
probably gets as many foreign visitors as any chemist in the world, people are
forever becoming adamant at the thought of accepting a substitute for the
brand they're used to.

25 'I'd often like to ask exactly what they're buying something *for*,' another
chemist says. 'They've read an ad, or a friend has recommended something.
Sometimes they're obviously buying a brand medicine to treat a condition they
should go to their doctor about. But you can't really ask people: they think
you're being inquisitive.'

30 His shop, one in a major chemists' group, has a big display of an iron preparation. These are usually aimed at women, women being more subject to
anaemia than men, although good diet avoids this to a large extent in middle-
class women. Patent medicines generally are rarely aimed at the top groups
in the social structure: advertising is placed largely in the tabloid press and in

**A medicine given to humour rather than cure a patient.*

continue overleaf

35 inexpensive women's magazines. 'Women come in asking for one of the iron preparations,' says the chemist. 'And nine out of ten of those who talk about why they have decided to take it say it's because they're—oh, "run down" or "tired" or depressed—something like that. Only one in ten or so says it's because she's recently been ill, or in hospital, or that iron deficiency has been
40 diagnosed.'

If you *are*, oh, tired/depressed/run down/ headachy/growing older, you can find plenty of over-the-counter proprietary medicines to match your vague symptoms: you pay your money, and you take your choice. In the advertising agent's proud cliché, 'Advertising allows you to choose.'

45 Advertising ethics now forbid adamant mass diagnosis by manufacturers. They don't say, if you're feeling run down, it must be because of nerves/constipation/indigestion/tension/vitamin deficiency—they say it *may* be.

Although there are many controls on terminology—largely voluntary until recently—the old meaningless words are there to match the meaningless
50 symptoms: 'tired blood,' 'restless legs,' 'nerves,' often in inverted commas. The survival of meaningless terms to describe non-specific symptoms is to some extent fed by doctors, who assume that their patients are incapable of understanding anything more specific—and/or are offering a *placebo* on the bitter grounds that you're only there for the cheer. 'My doctor says I need
55 a tonic,' says a typist. Has her doctor really used this word, unspecified? A housewife says importantly, 'I'm under the doctor for depression.' Has her doctor told her this, or has she interpreted what he's said? It seems that a lot of paternalistic doctors do offer such words to certain patients. In doing so, they're simply laying the patient wide open to the most flashy advertising.

60 If over-the-counter medicines harmlessly console people, and keep the doctors' surgeries from being crammed with *placebo*-seeking patients, they're justifiable. And the costly gloss of advertising is an essential part of such products. The trouble is, you may start reaching for medicines at the slightest discomfort—even for, say, depression caused by a depressing happening or
65 circumstance.

People involved in the advertising, or promotion, of a product have a specialised way of viewing television advertisements. That is to say, they actually listen to what's being said. To them, it's a concert of sight and sound. And your 'adman' refuses to believe that people don't listen; he'd fall on his
70 sword after admitting it. Anyway, it's an *advertisement*, I was told continually. People take ads with a pinch of salt. 'We credit people with a certain amount of common sense,' agents said reproachfully.

Is an assumption of 'common sense' in the average television ad-viewer a fair assumption?

75 Even if, as Peter Woodhouse suggests, there is a sort of middle-class mystique operating against patent medicines, this still leaves the probable average potential consumer of them—reachable through advertisements—as usually female, often in charge of a family, fairly uneducated and with poor dietary information. As such, she's certainly no more likely to be taking in the

46

80 theme of an advertisement than the rest of us. And there are others not educated to evaluate claims or symptoms.

Jane Alexander, 'As Good as a Tonic',
New Society

1 The first paragraph suggests clearly that Scott's Emulsion

- **A** has a harsh, unattractive pack
- **B** can be bought only at chain chemists
- **C** helps those who like fishing
- **D** is a traditional medicine
- **E** attracts only those who are poor

2 The chemist agrees that he likes Scott's Emulsion because it

- **A** is particularly good for him
- **B** contains a lot of rich ingredients
- **C** reminds him of when he was young
- **D** provides him with an income from its sale
- **E** has a very attractive, appetising smell

3 The claims on the Scott's Emulsion pack suggest that its main contribution to health lies in its

- **A** skin-improving qualities
- **B** vitamins and strength-giving properties
- **C** bone-building ingredients
- **D** whole-food characteristics
- **E** richness and easily-digestible contents

4 Which of the following means most nearly the same as 'buoyant' as it is used in line 14?

- **A** Common
- **B** Exaggerated
- **C** Emphatic
- **D** Fluent
- **E** Reassuring

5 'Notoriously' (line 15) suggests that new patent medicines are difficult to market because

- **A** the public prefers those it knows and trusts
- **B** criminal elements quickly exploit them
- **C** they soon manage to attract bad reputations
- **D** competition is too great amongst salesmen
- **E** they are not available on prescription

continue overleaf

6 The description of the chemist as a *placebo* (line 16) implies that he is

  A quick to sell a reassuring medicine
  B able to win his customers' confidence
  C successful because of his hard work
  D more skilled than most doctors
  E experienced in diagnosing what is needed

7 Since the start of prescription charges, chemists have found that elderly and poor people

  A visit their own doctors when they are ill
  B save money by refusing to pay prescription costs
  C decide on their illness and its treatment by themselves
  D rely on patent medicines rather than the Health Service
  E discuss how much they should pay with the chemist

8 Which of the following is nearest in meaning to 'adamant' as it is used in line 23 ?

  A Unpleasant
  B Immovable
  C Suspicious
  D Reluctant
  E Apprehensive

9 According to the article, people buy patent medicines for all of the following reasons EXCEPT that they

  A prefer something which they know
  B have been influenced by advertising
  C can get no medical treatment as foreigners
  D would rather not visit their own doctor
  E have been told they are good by a friend

10 Advertisements for patent medicines are usually aimed at

  1 readers of women's magazines
  2 members of the upper classes
  3 buyers of popular newspapers
  4 men suffering from anaemia

  A 1 and 2 only
  B 1 and 3 only
  C 2 and 3 only
  D 2 and 4 only
  E 3 and 4 only

48

11 Those who buy iron preparations rarely do so because they

- A get tired easily and quickly
- B feel generally unwell
- C begin to feel old
- D have an iron deficiency
- E are genuinely run down

12 Which of the following is nearest in meaning to 'cliché' as it is used in line 44?

- A Ill-founded boast
- B Slogan
- C Well-worn saying
- D Falsehood
- E Well-authenticated claim

13 According to the article, advertisers of patent medicines no longer

- A make use of vague, empty phrases which are unscientific
- B exploit people with vague symptoms of illness
- C claim to be able to tell people what is wrong with them
- D encourage people to make a choice between available medicines
- E present their material to the masses in popular publications

14 It is suggested that doctors sometimes use vague language to their patients because they believe those they treat often

- A prefer not to know the truth about their illness
- B like to enjoy sympathy others show them
- C cannot remember what is said to them anyway
- D need only a placebo in fact to comfort them
- E are unable to grasp technical medical language

15 The two questions in lines 55-7 indicate that the writer

- A realises patients tend to simplify their doctors' comments for themselves
- B thinks that the typist and housewife are both liars
- C cannot believe doctors would really behave like that
- D wishes to show what advertising can achieve
- E knows that women are more imprecise than men

16 'Paternalistic' (line 58) suggests that such doctors are

- A misleading
- B condescending
- C aristocratic
- D incompetent
- E misguided

continue overleaf

17 According to the passage, medicines given to humour rather than to cure patients have the one real social advantage of

    A   helping workers in the packaging industry
    B   keeping television advertisers in work
    C   creating a universal dependence on medicines
    D   making people think clearly about drugs
    E   relieving pressure on hard-working doctors

18 Those responsible for advertising on television insist on working on the assumption that

    A   they alone can really appreciate commercials
    B   sound is more important than what is shown
    C   they will have to listen to the public's criticism
    D   viewers pay attention to the contents of advertisements
    E   commercials are not to be taken seriously by anyone

19 The expression 'he'd fall on his sword' (lines 69–70) means that he would

    A   put away his sword to take up his pen
    B   become very aggressive towards attackers
    C   prefer to die rather than live
    D   put up a defence against all criticism
    E   be as cutting as he possibly could

20 The last paragraph suggests that we are vulnerable to advertisements for patent medicines for all of the following reasons EXCEPT that

    A   we allow our middle-class prejudices to operate
    B   we do not understand medical terminology
    C   we fail to listen to the commercials
    D   we are ignorant about what we should eat
    E   we find it hard to judge for ourselves

Now go back and check your work

Development

Further reading
E. Waugh's *The Loved One*, an amusing account of elaborate funeral customs in America bought by mourners for a number of improbable or unworthy reasons.

Discussion

How far should the government censor advertisements?
What standards of practice should advertisers be expected to observe?
How do advertisements enrich or detract from the quality of our lives?

Essays

The strangest advertisement in the world.
Advertisements which have influenced you.

Activity

Make a survey of TV advertising of patent medicines (or cosmetics, or tooth-paste). Look carefully for the methods used by advertisers (visual attractions, jingles, repetition, confident announcers, attempts to make the viewer feel deficient in some way so that he will buy the product, etc.).

It was the strangest murder trial I ever attended. They named it the Peckham
murder in the headlines, though Northwood Street, where the old woman
was found battered to death, was not strictly speaking in Peckham. This was
not one of those cases of circumstantial evidence, in which you feel the jury-
5 men's anxiety—because mistakes *have* been made—like domes of silence
muting the court. No, this murderer was all but found with the body; no one
present when the Crown counsel outlined his case believed that the man in the
dock stood any chance at all.

He was a heavy stout man with bulging bloodshot eyes. All his muscles
10 seemed to be in his thighs. Yes, an ugly customer, one you wouldn't forget in
a hurry—and that was an important point because the Crown proposed to call
four witnesses who hadn't forgotten him, who had seen him hurrying away
from the little red villa in Northwood Street. The clock had just struck two in
the morning.

15 Mrs Salmon in 15 Northwood Street had been unable to sleep; she heard a
door click shut and thought it was her own gate. So she went to the window
and saw Adams (that was his name) on the steps of Mrs Parker's house. He
had just come out and he was wearing gloves. He had a hammer in his hand
and she saw him drop it into the laurel bushes by the front gate. But before he
20 moved away, he had looked up—at her window. The fatal instinct that tells a
man when he is watched exposed him in the light of a street-lamp to her gaze
—his eyes suffused with horrifying and brutal fear, like an animal's when you
raise a whip. I talked afterwards to Mrs Salmon, who naturally after the
astonishing verdict went in fear herself. As I imagine did all the witnesses—
25 Henry MacDougall, who had been driving home from Benfleet late and
nearly ran Adams down at the corner of Northwood Street. Adams was
walking in the middle of the road looking dazed. And old Mr Wheeler, who
lived next door to Mrs Parker, at No. 12, and was wakened by a noise—like
a chair falling—through the thin-as-paper villa wall, and got up and looked
30 out of the window, just as Mrs Salmon had done, saw Adams's back and, as
he turned, those bulging eyes. In Laurel Avenue he had been seen by yet another witness—his luck was badly out; he might as well have committed the
crime in broad daylight.

'I understand,' counsel said, 'that the defence proposes to plead mistaken
35 identity. Adams's wife will tell you that he was with her at two in the morning
on February 14, but after you have heard the witnesses for the Crown and

examined carefully the features of the prisoner, I do not think you will be prepared to admit the possibility of a mistake.'

It was all over, you would have said, but the hanging.

40   After the formal evidence had been given by the policeman who had found the body and the surgeon who examined it, Mrs Salmon was called. She was the ideal witness, with her slight Scotch accent and her expression of honesty, care and kindness.

The counsel for the Crown brought the story gently out. She spoke very
45   firmly. There was no malice in her, and no sense of importance at standing there in the Central Criminal Court with a judge in scarlet hanging on her words and the reporters writing them down. Yes, she said, and then she had gone downstairs and rung up the police station.

'And do you see the man here in court?'
50   She looked straight at the big man in the dock, who stared hard at her with his pekingese eyes without emotion.

'Yes,' she said, 'there he is.'

'You are quite certain?'

She said simply, 'I couldn't be mistaken, sir.'
55   It was all as easy as that.

'Thank you, Mrs Salmon.'

Counsel for the defence rose to cross-examine. If you had reported as many murder trials as I have, you would have known beforehand what line he would take. And I was right, up to a point.
60   'Now, Mrs Salmon, you must remember that a man's life may depend on your evidence.'

'I do remember it, sir.'

'Is your eyesight good?'

'I have never had to wear spectacles, sir.'
65   'You are a woman of fifty-five?'

'Fifty-six, sir.'

'And the man you saw was on the other side of the road?'

'Yes, sir.'

'And it was two o'clock in the morning. You must have remarkable eyes,
70   Mrs Salmon?'

'No, sir. There was moonlight, and when the man looked up, he had the lamplight on his face.'

'And you have no doubt whatever that the man you saw is the prisoner?'

I couldn't make out what he was at. He couldn't have expected any other
75   answer than the one he got.

'None whatever, sir. It isn't a face one forgets.'

Counsel took a look round the court for a moment. Then he said, 'Do you mind, Mrs Salmon, examining again the people in court? No, not the prisoner. Stand up, please, Mr Adams,' and there at the back of the court, with thick
80   stout body and muscular legs and a pair of bulging eyes, was the exact image

continue overleaf

of the man in the dock. He was even dressed the same—tight blue suit and striped tie.

'Now think very carefully, Mrs Salmon. Can you still swear that the man you saw drop the hammer in Mrs Parker's garden was the prisoner—and not
85 this man, who is his twin brother?'

Of course she couldn't. She looked from one to the other and didn't say a word.

There the big brute sat in the dock with his legs crossed, and there he stood too at the back of the court and they both stared at Mrs Salmon. She shook
90 her head.

What we saw then was the end of the case. There wasn't a witness prepared to swear that it was the prisoner he'd seen. And the brother? He had his alibi, too; he was with his wife.

And so the man was acquitted for lack of evidence. But whether—if he did
95 the murder and not his brother—he was punished or not, I don't know. That extraordinary day had an extraordinary end. I followed Mrs Salmon out of court and we got wedged in the crowd who were waiting, of course, for the twins. The police tried to drive the crowd away, but all they could do was keep the roadway clear for traffic. I learned later that they tried to get the
100 twins to leave by a back way, but they wouldn't. One of them—no one knew which—said, 'I've been acquitted, haven't I?' and they walked bang out of the front entrance. Then it happened. I don't know how; though I was only six feet away. The crowd moved and somehow one of the twins got pushed on to the road right in front of a bus.

105 He gave a squeal like a rabbit and that was all; he was dead, his skull smashed just as Mrs Parker's had been. Divine vengeance? I wish I knew. There was the other Adams getting on his feet from beside the body and looking straight over at Mrs Salmon. He was crying, but whether he was the murderer or the innocent man, nobody will ever be able to tell. But if you were
110 Mrs Salmon, could you sleep at night?

Graham Greene, 'The Case for the Defence', *Collected Stories*

1 For which ONE of the following reasons was the Peckham murder trial probably the strangest that the author ever attended?

A Death struck dramatically to confuse the issue
B The criminal was finally acquitted
C Circumstantial evidence was produced
D The prosecution could not prove its case
E Mistaken identity was the main plea of the defence

2 'Circumstantial evidence' (line 4) given in court is evidence which

    A   can never be proved as being true
    B   may be inferred from known facts hard to explain
    C   can never be introduced into a trial
    D   is intended to deceive a jury
    E   can be adapted to suit the case

3 The anxiety of the jurymen described in lines 4–6 occurred most probably because they were afraid they might be

    A   condemning an innocent man
    B   stopped from hearing all the facts
    C   releasing a known murderer
    D   unable to make up their minds
    E   incapable of understanding the evidence

4 'Crown counsel' (line 7) is the barrister who speaks for the

    A   court
    B   witnesses
    C   jury
    D   prosecution
    E   defence

5 The chances of the accused man's being acquitted were thought to be very slight because

    A   the Crown counsel was very clever
    B   he did not seem to have an alibi
    C   the police found him near the murder
    D   he looked such an evil and violent man
    E   the witnesses had seen him quite clearly

6 Which of the following was not expected to appear as a witness in the case?

    A   Mrs Salmon
    B   Adams's wife
    C   Henry MacDougall
    D   Mrs Parker
    E   Mr Wheeler

continue overleaf

7 Which of the following is nearest in meaning to 'suffused' as it is used in line 22?

A Fixed
B Welling
C Protruding
D Bloodshot
E Shut

8 The author thought that all the witnesses probably 'went in fear' (line 24) after the verdict because they were afraid of

A vengeance from the accused
B being punished by divine justice
C prosecution for perjuring themselves
D disbelieving their own senses in future
E conscience plaguing them for ever

9 It is suggested that Adams 'might as well have committed the crime in broad daylight' (lines 32–3) because he

A had been seen by so many people
B would have been able to see better
C had a good chance of being proved innocent
D would have been able to murder the witnesses
E had succeeded in leaving the murder-scene

10 The Crown's case seemed to rest on proving that

1 the witnesses had seen him
2 he had been caught in the act
3 his face was unmistakable
4 he had obviously used a hammer
5 Mrs Salmon was a reliable witness

A 1, 2 and 3 only
B 1, 2 and 4 only
C 1, 3 and 5 only
D 2, 3 and 4 only
E 3, 4 and 5 only

11 Adams's eyes are described as 'pekingese' (line 51) because their main characteristic was that they were

A red
B bulging
C cold
D tearful
E enormous

56

12 The writer expected the defence counsel to take a line which would

    A   suggest that Mrs Salmon's observation was not completely reliable
    B   persuade the jury to feel sorry for the murderer
    C   show that the crime was not in Adams's nature
    D   emphasise the gravity of the crime committed
    E   prove that the case was one of suicide

13 All of the following answers of Mrs Salmon did not help the defence counsel
EXCEPT

    A   'I do remember it, sir.' (line 62)
    B   'I have never had to wear spectacles, sir.' (line 64)
    C   'Fifty-six, sir.' (line 66)
    D   'No, sir. There was moonlight.' (line 71)
    E   'None whatever, sir. It isn't a face one forgets.' (line 76)

14 Counsel most probably made the remark 'No, not the prisoner' (line 78)
because

    A   Adams had stood up to be recognised
    B   Mrs Salmon was still looking at Adams
    C   Adams thought he was being addressed
    D   Mrs Salmon seemed to see Adams's face everywhere
    E   Adams was obviously the real criminal

15 The most likely reason why Mrs Salmon 'didn't say a word' (lines 86–7) after
seeing Adams's twin was that she was

    A   ashamed
    B   excited
    C   angry
    D   confused
    E   suspicious

16 Lines 88–9 suggest that

    A   the twins were constantly changing position
    B   Adams's spirit seemed to move from body to body
    C   the defence had arranged some kind of trick
    D   some occult happening was actually taking place
    E   Mrs Salmon thought she was seeing double

continue overleaf

17 Which of the following is nearest in meaning to 'alibi' as it is used in line 92?

    A   Freedom from guilt
    B   Excuse for the crime
    C   Evidence of being elsewhere
    D   Moment of suspicion
    E   Chance to give testimony

18 Adams was finally acquitted of the charge against him because

    A   he had been far too clever for the prosecution
    B   no evidence at all had been produced
    C   his brother's alibi confused the jury
    D   none of the evidence conclusively proved his guilt
    E   he had managed convincingly to prove he was innocent

19 'Punished' (line 95) suggests that Adams might have been

    A   divinely repaid
    B   conscience-stricken
    C   subsequently hanged
    D   driven insane
    E   deliberately murdered

20 All of the following are incontestable facts in the case EXCEPT that the

    A   murderer left the scene of the crime after 2.00 a.m.
    B   victim was an old lady living next door to Mr Wheeler
    C   murder had been committed by one of the Adams twins
    D   crime took place just outside the Peckham district
    E   person who had been murdered had been battered to death

Now go back and check your work

Development

Further reading

G. Greene, *Twenty-one Stories* (Penguin). This collection includes 'The Basement Room', made into a film, *The Fallen Idol*, with Sir Ralph Richardson as its star. The story deals with the shattered illusions of a small boy. Another story, 'The Destructors', is equally terrifying in describing the motiveless destruction of an old man's house by The Wormsley Common Gang.

Discussion

Consider the part played by the police in bringing a prosecution. You may be able to persuade a police officer to visit the school to give you information and join in the discussion.

How far do you think society should punish or try to rehabilitate offenders? What are meant by *crime* and *punishment*?

Written work

Write a report on your discussions or attempt a short story which takes as its main theme the detection of a crime.

Write an essay on 'Anti-social behaviour in the (school) community'.

Activities

Arrange a visit to the local Magistrates' Court or to a higher court of justice. For a visit to the Crown Court (formerly the Quarter Sessions) you should write to the Chief Clerk of the Court; for a visit to the local Magistrates' Court you should write to the Clerk to the Justices. In both cases you must write well in advance of the visit to seek approval and confirmation that the court will be sitting. From the public gallery you will be able to follow the procedures easily and listen to cases for the prosecution and the defence.

Obtain reports from two different newspapers of a day's proceedings at an important trial. Examine them carefully and make lists of similar points given in each and of points which occur in one but not in another. Then, using the lists, write a brief summary of the day's events from the point of view of either a friendly or a hostile witness.

The Hazards

London's great smog in 1952 when hundreds of people died demonstrated savagely how air pollution could endanger health. Thanks to the official action that followed, air pollutants, with one glaring exception, are now lesser causes of illness and death than they were twenty years ago.

5   The exception? Cigarette smoke—when it is self-administered. Smoking is a more significant cause of premature death and disabling illness than any other form of air pollution.

After cigarettes—and since the Clean Air Act it comes a long way after—coal smoke is the most serious hazard. Sudden and severe exposure, as used
10   to occur during smog, carried a fatal risk for the weaker members of the community—the newborn, the old and frail, and those already suffering from chest or heart disease. By irritating the lining of the bronchial tubes and the much smaller airways that carry air into the substance of the lungs, smoke stimulates the production of large quantities of phlegm which can be cleared
15   only by repeated and forcible coughing. In patients whose lung capacity is taxed to the full because of heart failure or chest disease, this energetic coughing is not only exhausting but can be fatal.

People who breathe air polluted with smoke for most of their lives are more likely than others to develop chronic bronchitis, the progressively worsening
20   lung disease that kills over 30,000 people in the United Kingdom each year. Cigarette smoking again plays its part by thickening the lining of the airways in the lung, making them narrower and breathing more difficult, and by stimulating the production of phlegm and the coughing needed to get rid of it. Laboratory experiments have shown that coal-smoke deposits in the lung
25   stimulate the growth of bacteria, and coal smoke's contribution to chronic bronchitis is probably to encourage bacteria to move into cigarette-affected lungs and cause infection and destruction of tissue. Since the passing of the Clean Air Act in 1956, the death rate from chronic bronchitis in industrial cities has been dropping nearer to that in rural areas.

30   Despite the strong evidence that smoke causes chest disease, the experts still cannot tell us which of its ingredients do the damage. Only one—the grit and dust fall-out—can be exonerated; the particles are too big to be inhaled into the smaller airways of the lungs where the most severe damage occurs.

60

35 Three other ingredients are potential dangers: sulphur dioxide, produced
by burning coal, coke, and heavy oils; sulphuric acid, produced when sulphur
dioxide combines with the water in the atmosphere; and the smoke itself,
which consists of dust particles too small to fall out.

Sulphur dioxide is an undoubted irritant. Sulphuric acid is a possible
40 irritant but, in droplet form, is diluted by secretions in the bronchial tubes
and does little damage. Workers in battery factories, for instance, are often
exposed to sulphuric acid mist, yet seem no more susceptible than other people
to chest disease. When sulphuric acid gets stuck on to solid particles, however,
it can be inhaled deep into the lungs and set up intense irritation.

The Legal Position

45 The 1956 Clean Air Act and a second, strengthening, measure in 1968 have
made major contributions to the fight against air pollution.

(1) They have enabled local authorities to make 'smokeless zones' where
only authorised smokeless fuels may be burned or specifically exempted substantially smoke-free fireplaces used. 4,702,082 premises and 948,559 acres
50 are affected. Maximum penalty for each individual infringement is a £20 fine.
When a new zone is made, the local authority has to pay at least 70 per cent
of the reasonable cost of converting existing fireplaces in houses built before
August, 1964—and may, at its own discretion, pay the lot.

(2) Whether or not a smoke control order is in force, dark and black smoke
55 may only be emitted from industrial chimneys (which must be of an approved
height) at a specific standard rate throughout the country—i.e. only four
minutes of dark smoke (except when caused by soot blowing) at any one time,
no more than two minutes of black smoke in any given half-hour Penalty for
an offender: a fine of up to £100.

60 (3) Apart from smoke from chimneys, dark smoke cannot be emitted from
any part of industrial or trade premises—for example, trade refuse burnt in
the open—without the occupier being liable to a £100 fine.

But the Clean Air Acts cannot be enforced by the ordinary citizen. Only
local authorities are empowered to bring prosecutions. You can, of course,
complain to the local authority, but it is entirely their decision whether to go
65 ahead with a magistrates' court summons or to try to deal with the case by
negotiation and persuasion. And there is practically no effective law against
pollution of the atmosphere from motor vehicle exhausts.

Michael O'Donnell, 'Is Breathing Dangerous?',
The Sunday Times Magazine

1 An example given in the passage of the way air pollution can endanger health is the

    A   large number of premises affected by the smokeless zones order
    B   passing of the Clean Air Act by Parliament in 1956
    C   dirty fall-out from factory chimneys in the cities
    D   great smog which descended on London in 1952
    E   large number of people who continue to smoke cigarettes

2 According to the article, the most important cause of premature death by air pollution is the smoke from

    1   car exhausts
    2   coal
    3   burning refuse
    4   cigarettes

    A   1 and 2 only
    B   1 and 3 only
    C   2 and 3 only
    D   2 and 4 only
    E   3 and 4 only

3 The people most likely to be killed by smog will be those who are

    1   smoking many cigarettes
    2   newly born
    3   suffering from heart disease
    4   old and feeble
    5   working in factories

    A   1, 2 and 4 only
    B   1, 3 and 5 only
    C   2, 3 and 4 only
    D   2, 3 and 5 only
    E   3, 4 and 5 only

4 Air pollution can cause sudden death by

    A   swamping the lungs with bacteria so that they suddenly stop
    B   irritating the linings of the lungs which then refuse to work
    C   stimulating the rapid production of phlegm which fills the lungs
    D   creating acids which quickly attack and eat away the lungs
    E   bringing on violent coughing when the lungs are already fully taxed

5 'Chronic bronchitis' (line 19) is an illness which

    A   lasts for some time
    B   is always fatal
    C   arises inevitably from cigarette smoking
    D   is constantly painful
    E   exists only in the cities and towns

6 Chronic bronchitis involves all the following EXCEPT

    A   coughing up lung tissue
    B   bacteria in the lungs
    C   infection of lung tissue
    D   increasing deterioration of the lungs
    E   destruction of lung tissue

7 Chronic bronchitis affects

    A   only those living in industrial cities
    B   some people living in cities and country areas
    C   very heavy cigarette smokers only
    D   all those working in battery factories
    E   only those who suffer from weak hearts

8 Which of the following is nearest in meaning to 'exonerated' as it is used in line 32?

    A   Measured with accuracy
    B   Controlled
    C   Freed from blame
    D   Ignored
    E   Picked out clearly

9 Two factors which can cause chronic bronchitis are thought to be

    1   grit and dust in the lungs arising from city smoke
    2   forced coughing brought about by smoke in the air
    3   lung airways becoming thickened due to cigarette smoke
    4   bacteria growing in the lungs encouraged by coal smoke

    A   1 and 2 only
    B   1 and 3 only
    C   2 and 3 only
    D   2 and 4 only
    E   3 and 4 only

continue overleaf

10 One effect of the 1956 Clean Air Act has been

A   a fall in the number of deaths from chronic bronchitis
B   the elimination of sulphur dioxide from the atmosphere
C   a fall in the pollutants coming from vehicle exhausts
D   the elimination of dust particles from the atmosphere
E   a fall in the number of people smoking cigarettes

11 As it leaves the furnaces industrial smoke contains all of the following EXCEPT

A   dust which falls to the ground
B   sulphur dioxide
C   grit which falls to the ground
D   sulphuric acid
E   dust which remains permanently floating

12 Dangerous lung irritants found in industrial smoke include

1   sulphur dioxide
2   bacteria
3   floating particles of dust
4   heavy oils

A   1 and 2 only
B   1 and 3 only
C   2 and 3 only
D   2 and 4 only
E   3 and 4 only

13 The passage suggests that houses in 'smokeless zones' since 1964 have been built

A   with fireplaces that burned smokeless fuel
B   without any chimneys
C   with local authority subsidies for fireplaces
D   without any grates
E   with central heating from boilers

14 The passage makes it clear that a shop-keeper burning rubbish causing black smoke may

A   be fined £100 no matter how little the black smoke
B   have his premises closed by the local authority
C   be fined a maximum of £20 for each offence
D   have to change his equipment to smokeless burners
E   be fined £100 for more than two minutes of black smoke

64

15 Prosecutions under the 1956 Clean Air Act can be brought by

  A local authorities
  B Parliament
  C private citizens
  D doctors
  E local magistrates

16 Which of the following is nearest in meaning to 'at its own discretion' as it is used in line 53 ?

  A In its official position
  B By a special law
  C Out of its good nature
  D As it sees fit
  E From its own funds

17 In the fight against air pollution the ordinary citizen can

  A force the police to send official warnings under the Clean Air Act
  B bring private prosecutions
  C insist that his Member of Parliament issues a summons
  D do nothing useful
  E report breaches of the Clean Air Act to his local authority

18 To enforce the 1956 Clean Air Act local councils can use all the following EXCEPT

  A magistrates' courts
  B negotiation
  C police arrests
  D persuasion
  E court summonses

19 Under the 1956 Clean Air Act local councils can do all of the following EXCEPT

  A bring prosecutions against people
  B close offending factories and shop premises
  C set up smokeless zones
  D pay towards the cost of altering fireplaces
  E take up complaints from private individuals

20 A major source of air pollution unaffected by the 1956 Clean Air Act is

  A factory chimneys
  B the burning of factory waste
  C car exhausts
  D the burning of shop refuse
  E domestic fireplaces

Now go back and check your work

65

Development

Discussion

What is the connection between smoking and illness? Perhaps the School doctor might be persuaded to introduce a discussion on this topic. Local health centres will be able to provide you with facts, figures, and diagrams. What will be the sources of fuel and heat in a hundred years' time?

Essays

Describe a campaign designed to stop people from smoking.

Sickness in the family.

Scents and stinks.

'Air pollution will make cities impossible to live in eventually.' How far do you agree?

Projects

Local levels of pollution.

Your local medical services.

Careers in medicine or the social services.

TEST 10

Read the passage. Then answer the questions. Do not guess.

According to my mother, tradesmen had the best jobs in the world. They were independent of any one employer, and, more important, of any one town. Once a lad had served his time he could always try some other job, knowing that failure wouldn't be the end of the world. As far as Mother was concerned,
5 a trade was the finest personal insurance policy in the world. And I can understand why. She hated my Dad working shifts in the glass-works in St Helens. She hated the fact that he was tied down to one employer and one town. Dad was more sceptical about tradesmen, partly because he'd seen some so-called trades eliminated at Pilkington's. He felt that the technicians, who were
10 beginning to emerge in the glass-works, would be the tradesmen of the future. And the super-tradesmen were the applied scientists. But the general attitude was that lads should be working at sixteen. If they were bright they could get their qualifications at night-school. And in the meantime they could pay their way at home and put something into the family budget. Keeping kids was one
15 thing, keeping a young adult in clothes, shoes and spends was another. This was a regular theme with the gossips at the Co-op. 'They never do their parents any good,' they'd say, meaning that the college-educated child never made a contribution to the running of the house—never 'tipped up', never paid board. They were away and married, only came back to scandalise their
20 parents with their posh talk and hoity-toity ways. There was only one thing for it: get 'em into a good trade and forget all about fancy education.

At fifteen, half my friends left school to get themselves into apprenticeships. I stuck it out for another couple of years into the sixth form, and then I dropped out into a trade and onto a building site. It was a switch from
25 calculus, the theory of valency and the principle of the conservation of energy to the medieval overtones of the deeds of apprenticeship. But I learnt a trick or two.

My first job was to brew tea. Then a tall plasterer named Alf Smith, who looked like a local version of Lee Marvin, handed me an empty putty-drum
30 and a spike-headed hammer and told me to make a brazier and get a coke fire going. I took the putty-drum outside and nipped into the next house to examine their brazier. It was perfectly round with a regular series of holes punched in it, large at the bottom and small at the top. I marched back to my unblemished drum and gave it a sharp belt in the middle with the pointed end
35 of the hammer. Disaster: the whole side of the drum caved in and there was

continue overleaf

67

only one microscopic puncture in the metal. I tried to straighten the side back into shape by forcing my foot into the drum. Gradually I prised down on the indentation—and my foot shot through to the bottom. Immediately the metal sprang back, trapping my leg. I couldn't force it apart with my hands so I
40 clomped across the road and forced the handle of a spade into the drum and withdrew my leg. It was bleeding.

Next I grabbed a spar about six foot long, wedged the drum under the wheel of a concrete mixer and began levering the crumpled side into shape. Then suddenly the opposite side of the drum collapsed and I landed on my
45 back in a puddle. By this time I was fighting mad and hammered blow after blow on the drum. It wilted, warped, and flattened. It was only then I realised that I had an audience: the new gang of plasterers had been watching the performance from the sanctuary of the houses. Some of them were almost speechless with laughter. I was so angry I felt I could burst. Alf Smith came loping
50 out of the house with a new putty-drum. 'That was a technical piece of artistry if ever I saw it,' he said. He took me across to where the sand was stored and carefully filled the drum with sand. Then, with a series of light taps with the hammer, he punched a neat line of holes in the side of the drum, without a fraction of distortion. As I carried the completed brazier back to the house, Alf
55 asked me whether I knew the difference between a wise man and a fool. 'A wise man knows what he doesn't know and a fool doesn't. And you can tell a wise man because he'll ask when he doesn't know and a fool won't. OK?'

When the gang was working on ceilings the most junior apprentice— namely, me—would mix the plaster, move the scaffolds, and work on the
60 trowel when the plaster began its final set. The plaster used on the ceilings was specially treated to set slowly. I'd take half a bucket of water to where the plaster was stored, fill it to the brim with the powder and leave it to soak for a couple of minutes. Then I'd beat it to a fine cream with a mixing stick. After a couple of months I'd learned a few dodges. I found out that a bucket mixed
65 with dirty water or a handful of dust thrown in it would set very quickly. On the other hand, a couple of cups of cold tea could delay the set for hours. Once I'd discovered this, the craftsmen I was working with only crossed me at their peril. Three quick fast-setting buckets of plaster would have them galloping frantically round the scaffold. A few slow-setting buckets kept them
70 at a ceiling long after everyone else had gone home.

At school you used words and ideas and numbers: 'things that went on in the front of your mind' is the best way I can express it. It was different serving an apprenticeship. You had to upgrade the way that your senses worked. Walking across a ceiling scaffold, you were constantly sensing the position
75 and the spring of the planks without looking down. Apprenticeship wasn't about this business of being bound to a master; it was about developing coordination, the ability to move materials without effort, and developing a sense of space.

I've talked to training managers in recent years who believe that the apprenticeship system should be scrapped. But I'm not sure whether this is right
80

68

for jobs that demand muscular strength, agility and staying power. From the age of fifteen to twenty, a person can develop an optimum muscle structure in relation to his job. And in the long run surely this makes the job easier for him. For me, it shouldn't have been a liberation from school—but it was. It
85 shouldn't have been the most vital part of my education—but it was.

Bob Houlton, 'My Apprenticeship', The Listener

1 The writer's mother believed that tradesmen had the best jobs in the world for all of the following reasons EXCEPT that they

    A   were not dependent on anyone
    B   had a secure job behind them for ever
    C   were assured of rapid promotion
    D   would find a job even away from home
    E   were free to explore other work

2 The writer's father did not share his wife's faith about learning a trade mainly because he

    A   believed newly educated scientists would see that tradesmen were eliminated
    B   had realised that outside the glassworks tradesmen had little future
    C   considered new industries required either machine-hands or scientists
    D   had already seen jobs labelled as 'trades' disappear in one company
    E   thought shift work was bound to destroy a man and his job

3 All of the following are objections given in the article to pupils' staying-on at school after sixteen EXCEPT

    A   young adults should help to pay for their keep
    B   night school provided opportunities for further education
    C   extra qualifications were really unnecessary in life
    D   youngsters with education very rarely thanked their parents
    E   older children should learn something useful and practical

4 'Scandalise' (line 19) suggests that the educated young people

    A   made their parents regret their own lost opportunities
    B   returned to tell their parents what to do with their lives
    C   talked to the neighbours about their own parents
    D   irritated their parents' circle of friends in many ways
    E   shocked their parents by what they said and did

continue overleaf

5 The writer was probably asked to brew the tea for the plasterers because they

    A knew he was good at it
    B thought it would keep him busy
    C had been told it was part of his job
    D gave this work traditionally to juniors
    E wanted him to have an easy time at first

6 The writer 'nipped into the next house to examine their brazier' (lines 31–2) to find out

    A how the holes were arranged
    B if theirs was round like his
    C whether he could borrow theirs
    D if he could get someone to help
    E how he should hold the hammer

7 'Microscopic' (line 36) suggests that the hole he had made was

    A uneven in shape
    B impossible to find
    C out of position
    D difficult to mend
    E hard to see

8 Which of the following means most nearly the same as 'prised' as it is used in line 37?

    A Forced
    B Stamped
    C Levered
    D Kicked
    E Squeezed

9 'Clomped' (line 40) suggests that his walk across the road was

    A dangerous
    B clumsy
    C secretive
    D painful
    E hurried

10 The author was 'fighting mad' (line 45) most probably because he

    A was frustrated at not being able to do the job
    B thought the plasterers were laughing at him
    C had hurt his leg which was bleeding
    D realised the men had played a joke on him
    E believed the time allowed had almost run out

11 'Wilted, warped, and flattened' (line 46) suggest that the final appearance of the drum was all of the following EXCEPT

    A   twisted
    B   jagged
    C   bent
    D   dented
    E   squashed

12 'Performance' (lines 47–8) suggests that his attempts had been

    A   planned beforehand by the author
    B   enjoyed by interested spectators
    C   dramatised like an actor's on a stage
    D   met with loud applause from the audience
    E   exaggerated in their violence

13 As Alf Smith appeared with the new putty-drum (lines 49–50) he

    A   was still speechless with laughter
    B   showed indifference to the boy's troubles
    C   took long, careless strides
    D   strolled lazily out from nowhere
    E   staggered under the drum's weight

14 When Alf Smith said, 'That was a technical piece of artistry if ever I saw it' (lines 50–1) he was being

    A   clever
    B   truthful
    C   disagreeable
    D   complimentary
    E   sarcastic

15 Alf Smith's distinction between a wise man and a fool (lines 55–7) depends on the fact that a wise man

    1   needs everything explained to him
    2   recognises his own ignorance
    3   distinguishes fools from clever men
    4   asks others who know more for help

    A   1 and 2 only
    B   1 and 3 only
    C   2 and 3 only
    D   2 and 4 only
    E   3 and 4 only

continue overleaf

16 The youngest member of the team of plasterers was expected to do all of the following EXCEPT

    A   shift the scaffolds
    B   prepare the plaster
    C   make the tea
    D   clean the tools
    E   light the fire

17 All of the following were steps in the preparation of properly mixed plaster EXCEPT

    A   adding the plaster to the water
    B   stirring the plaster with a clean stick
    C   allowing the plaster to soak up the water
    D   using half a bucket of water to a bucket of plaster
    E   mixing the plaster and water to a fine consistency

18 The writer found that the difference between being at school and being an apprentice lay mainly in the fact that at school it was a matter of

    A   obeying rules
    B   understanding theory
    C   having practical experience
    D   solving problems
    E   working with instructors

19 The writer concluded that he was largely in favour of an apprenticeship system because it

    1   occurred at a time when muscle-co-ordination was easily learnt
    2   gave the school-leaver a chance to make his own way in the world
    3   provided an escape into freedom from school for boys and girls
    4   allowed the young to acquire skills not acquired at school

    A   1 and 3 only
    B   1 and 4 only
    C   2 and 3 only
    D   2 and 4 only
    E   3 and 4 only

20 The last two sentences of the passage suggest strongly all of the following EXCEPT that Bob Houlton

    A   knew he was better than others
    B   felt disappointed with school
    C   enjoyed his apprenticeship
    D   continued to learn at work
    E   was free to find himself in a job

Now go back and check your work

Development

Discussion
What part should trades unions and employers play in apprenticeship? (You may be able to persuade a member of the local rotary club or a trade union representative to join you for the discussions.)
What are the responsibilities of a young person in accepting a job?

Essays
Work and play.
On leaving school.
Practical jokes and jokers.

Projects
Build up a file on the career you would like to follow. (This file should include pamphlets, advertisements for posts, information about working conditions, scope for future advancement, wages and salaries, responsibilities, rights trade union affiliation, etc.)

Activities
Arrange for your local Youth Employment Officer to visit your class to talk about apprenticeships today. Draw up a list of questions to put to him, including some which deal with personal relationships at work and day-release schemes which enable you to continue your education.
Invite some of last year's leavers to come back for a morning or afternoon to tell you about some of the problems they have found in starting work or going on to further education elsewhere.

The tide began to flow. The surface of the bay convulsed and then heaved its increase of water gracefully, with a sound like a deep sigh, against the low shore. The risen water paused and then receded, leaving a dark, wet flounce on the strips of sand. The weeds strained after it, taut and straight, like
5 fingers reaching for its touch.

The sound of the turning tide roused Sheila from a day-dream. She was sitting on the edge of the little concrete pier that jutted out into a corner of the bay. Her father's boat was moored, high and dry on the rocks, against the side of the pier. Her grey-haired father was in the bow, sewing a patch on the
10 net. It was afternoon towards the end of autumn, but the sun was strong. The heat of the sun and the silence of low tide had induced in her a torpor, within whose cloak she had woven a dream of passionate love.

A loud sound came from behind the low range of hills that bound the shore towards the east. Along the Galway road, which lay behind the hills, a cloud
15 of dust came moving rapidly. Then a large red bus appeared and halted by the entrance to the path that led from the road to the pier. A man descended from it.

'Oh! look, father,' she cried excitedly. 'A man got off the bus! He might be a tourist for the islands. He has a big stick in his hand, and a knapsack on his back and he's bareheaded. As sure as you are alive, he's an artist going out to
20 the islands.'

Her speech was now thick and halting. There was a hardness in her throat that forced her to swallow her breath after each few words.

'It's late in the year for anyone to be going out to the islands,' her father said. 'I haven't carried anyone out there now for more than a fortnight.'
25 As the stranger approached, Sheila noticed that he was handsome and her excitement increased. It was of such a man she had dreamt. He had a fine, arrogant carriage, like a soldier or someone in authority. When he reached the end of the pier, he addressed them in a rich, deep voice that disturbed her as the voluptuous rising of the tide had done.
30 'You're Bartley Manning, I'm told,' he said to her father.

'That's right,' said her father.

'The bus conductor told me you take people to the islands,' the man continued. 'I'd like to go there if you can take me.'

Her father examined the man from head to foot, shrewdly measuring his
35 capacity to pay. Then he said:

'When were you thinking of going?'

'Right away.'

'That's a different story, for my boatman is gone to Galway and he won't be back before tonight.'

40 'Oh!' said the stranger. 'That's too bad. You couldn't get someone else instead of him?'

'I would have to think hard,' he said gloomily, 'for it's not everyone would do for the job of going with me beyond the bay to the islands at this time of year.'

45 Sheila understood her father's manoeuvre and felt ashamed.

But he straightened himself suddenly, turned towards the stranger and cried in a menacing shout:

'It will be two pounds for the trip.'

The stranger smiled and said casually: 'That's all right.'

50 Her father's attitude changed at once. He became full of energy and a fawning grin creased his furrowed face, as he hitched up his trousers and said:

'I'll go right away up to the village and find a boy to go with me.'

'I think I'll wait here,' the stranger said.

Her father began to climb out on to the pier, crying excitedly:

55 'You won't have to wait long and my daughter there will chat with you. The boat'll swim in half an hour. It's spring tide and the sea comes belting in very quick. We can make the island on one tack with this fine breeze that's rising.'

Sheila felt terribly ashamed of her father as he clattered up the pier in his

60 hobnailed boots. His frieze trousers were very ragged, but he was a fine type of his fisher breed. The poor girl, drunk with romantic thoughts of captivating the handsome stranger, only saw his raggedness and his uncouth avarice. She was afraid that the stranger would despise her for having such a father.

'My goodness!' the stranger cried after her father had gone. 'What air!

65 What a scene! Lucky people that live here.' He stood with his arms outstretched, breathing deeply as he looked out over the landlocked bay. Sheila was disappointed. Somehow, she had felt certain that he would turn to her at once and pay her attention as soon as her father had gone.

'The sea is lovely, sure enough,' said Sheila sharply, 'but the land is awful.

70 I don't think it's lucky for anybody to live here in poverty.'

The stranger turned round, put his hands on his hips and looked inland.

'You think so?' he cried, passionately. 'I wish I lived here. I love this great Connemara desert. I've walked all over it. It's really a desert. There's only heather and stone growing out of the boggy earth. And yet it's full of wonders,

75 when you go walking there alone. It's lovely to see the steel ropes of the white waterfalls on the mountain sides and the ghostly light on the high-up stony peaks of the mountains. There is something in the air that walks with you and tries to talk to you, like music in a great empty room.'

But Sheila felt scorned and humiliated by this rapturous worship of the

80 earth, while he paid no heed to herself.

continue overleaf

'I hate it,' she said fiercely. 'I hate the living sight of it.'

The stranger looked at her in wonder.

With an effort, she restrained her tears and turned round. She saw her father and the boy coming down the path that led from the road to the pier.

85 'Oh!' said the stranger. 'Upon my soul, I had clean forgotten about the trip. Well! Here goes for a look at fairyland.'

He laughed heartily and strode over to the boat, which was now afloat, and got in. It was not yet quite clear of the rocks on which it had lain. It staggered, like a person trying to walk after a long illness, as its keel grated against the

90 rocks. It heaved angrily at the mooring ropes that halted it until it was released.

Her father began to sing at the helm. The stranger joined in the song. She listened to his singing voice in sad rapture, as it grew faint over the lengthening water. Tears flowed from her eyes and she felt utterly forlorn. She had a horrid feeling that this was the turning-point in her life, that she had missed her last

95 chance of happiness and that the future was going to be barren.

Liam O'Flaherty, 'The Lament', *Short Stories*

1 Which of the following is nearest in meaning to 'convulsed' as it is used in line 1 ?

   A   Curved away

   B   Shook violently

   C   Drew away

   D   Turned back

   E   Broke up

2 The visual effect of the receding tide on the bay's stones and strips of sand reminds the writer of a

   A   necklace round a woman's neck

   B   shiny fish found inshore

   C   strip of material edging a woman's skirt

   D   slender plant found near the coastline

   E   veil round the rim of a woman's hat

3 The way the weeds act in the receding tide reminds the author of the behaviour of

   A   insects

   B   fish

   C   reptiles

   D   people

   E   trees

4 Sheila's father appeared to earn his living from

   1   smuggling

   2   carrying tourists

   3   fishing

   4   carrying goods

76

A   1 and 2 only
B   1 and 3 only
C   2 and 3 only
D   2 and 4 only
E   3 and 4 only

5 Which of the following is nearest in meaning to 'torpor' as it is used in line 11 ?

A   Numbness
B   Confusion
C   Enthusiasm
D   Vision
E   Sensation

6 The hardness in Sheila's throat (line 21) was probably caused by the

A   fear of meeting an obvious stranger
B   need to put on her best speaking voice
C   greed arising from the chance of making money
D   anticipation of meeting a sensitive, lively artist
E   tension aroused in her by seeing an attractive man

7 The 'manoeuvre' (line 44) of which Sheila was ashamed was her father's

A   pretence that he did not understand the stranger's request
B   unwillingness to get up and walk into the village
C   attempt to frighten the stranger by shouting
D   exaggeration of the difficulties in order to raise his fee
E   desire to leave her alone with a possible husband

8 Sheila's father's shout is said to be 'menacing' (line 46) because he was

A   demanding a ridiculously high payment
B   frightened he would not be paid properly
C   threatening the voyage would be dangerous
D   uncertain how to behave in the circumstances
E   angry at having to make the dangerous journey

9 Sheila's father's boat was driven by

A   oars
B   sail
C   paddles
D   propeller
E   paddle-wheel

continue overleaf

10 The effect of a 'spring tide' (line 56) is said to

    A increase the speed of the water's movements
    B take the sea out further than usual
    C increase the warmth and activity of the sea
    D bring the sea further inland than usual
    E increase the depth of the sea

11 Sheila felt ashamed of her father because he was

    1 tattered in his appearance
    2 unscrupulous in getting money from the stranger
    3 likely to make the stranger look down on her
    4 too excited to sail his boat alone
    5 rude to the stranger who had arrived

    A 1, 2 and 3 only
    B 1, 2 and 5 only
    C 1, 3 and 4 only
    D 2, 4 and 5 only
    E 3, 4 and 5 only

12 A description of Sheila's father's appearance would include all of the following EXCEPT the fact that he

    A had grey hair
    B wore hobnailed boots
    C had a lined face
    D wore patched trousers
    E had a stooping walk

13 Which of the following is nearest in meaning to 'landlocked' as it is used in line 66?

    A In the centre of the country
    B Dried up
    C Almost enclosed by land
    D Cut off
    E Difficult to reach from the shore

14 The stranger called this part of Connemara a 'desert' (line 73) because it

    A was covered in sand dunes to the coast
    B inspired men to explore it
    C was remote from the rest of the world
    D created mirages in travellers' minds
    E was barren and treeless

15 The waterfalls are said to be 'steel ropes' (line 75) because they were all of the following EXCEPT

- A shiny
- B powerful
- C hard
- D descending
- E slender

16 In the Connemara desert the stranger seems to have liked all the following EXCEPT the

- A scenery
- B feeling in the atmosphere
- C waterfalls
- D light on the hilltops
- E people of the area

17 Features of the bay included all the following EXCEPT

- A a beach of sand
- B islands
- C hills along one side
- D rocks
- E a pier in one corner

18 In the passage Sheila experienced all of the following EXCEPT

- A excitement
- B shame
- C disappointment
- D humiliation
- E amusement

19 Sheila could best be described as

- A romantic
- B slovenly
- C unfeeling
- D cheerful
- E beautiful

20 Sheila appears to have been dominated by the idea of

- A rising to a high social position
- B how poor and ugly she was
- C meeting a potential husband before it was too late
- D how beautiful the sea was
- E getting away from Connemara to a big city

Now go back and check your work

Development

Discussion

How far does poverty make people brutal and cunning?

Are girls more romantic than boys?

What can be done to preserve the lonely and beautiful places of our country?

Essays

The mysterious island.

My most romantic (or outrageous) daydreams.

The role of women in the world today.

Continue the story from where the passage leaves off.

Projects

Hiking and rambling today. (If you wish, you might prefer to deal with another outdoor hobby—mountaineering, cycling, sailing, fishing, etc.)

'The street is going down.' This is one of those adult forebodings which haunted our childhoods and remains today, essentially unchanged. It seems to
express an obscure and often irrational dread, or a sense of personal ageing
and inadequacy which goes far beyond the actual street and the actual people
5 in it. You would think, to listen to the words they mutter to one another or to
themselves as Londoners walk the pavements, that in some golden age of
antiquity (situated, according to choice, before the second world war, before
the first one, before the cinemas were turned into bingo halls or the music halls
into cinemas), every area in London was nice—with a few agreed exceptions
10 such as the East End. Doorsteps, apparently, were always scrubbed, by
housewives, always honest and industrious, however poor; pavements were
continually swept by sober employees who took pride in their work; gardens
were tended and dogs, children and similar mess-makers kept in order.
This is a largely working-class view. There is a parallel one, precisely
15 contradicting it, which is held mainly by the upper-middle-class. In this
second view, the whole of inner London (excepting, again, certain well-
defined areas) was 'before the war' or 'up to 1950', one vast, faceless slum, or
at any rate limbo, inhabited mainly by men with mufflers and barrows,
women with curlers and children with runny noses who (the touchstone of
20 upper-middle-class disapproval) played in the streets.
A spurious credence is given to the 'used-to-be-a-slum' viewpoint by the
disproportionate boom in inner London property prices as these areas became
fashionable. Houses which, in the early fifties, were worth virtually nothing
now fetch between ten and twenty thousand pounds. The social transforma-
25 tion must, you might assume from this, be enormous—all those curlers and
mufflers and barrows or their modern equivalents swept away forever, and
nothing but window boxes and expensive cars as far as the eye can see. Such
has been the fate of L— Street, in northwest inner London, built in several
successive stages between 1830 and 1860. In the late 1950s you could still get
30 a house round here for a few hundred pounds; a garden, spacious living
accommodation, within twenty minutes' walk of central London. No more.

Inevitably, in spite of superficial appearances, these streets can only become
increasingly upper-middle-class—that is, less and less of a cohesive community, all dependent upon the same shops and schools. For what goes, when
continue overleaf

35 an area like L— Street gradually changes from a run-down one to a sought-
after one, is not only the working-class owner-occupiers but the incidental
tenants, both long- and short-term. Since most of these properties are sub-
divided, not only will future elderly spinsters find it impossible to acquire
property here, but there will be no rooms for future old boys seeking homely
40 digs and no cheap bedsitters for hard-up young men ('Share landlady's toilet
through kitchen'). The lost railings may be replaced, the broken windows
mended, the leaking slate-roofs taken off and put back again instead of being
kept in their place with blackback above and tin pails below but, though the
houses benefit, where will the ordinary people go? A basement with a broken
45 window, in the district you have known for years, can be better than a council
flat somewhere at the far end of nowhere, and vastly better than nowhere at
all. A small shop, if you are a small shop-keeper, at a rent you can afford and
with some rooms above it, is something which it is becoming harder and
harder to come by. They are demolished, and by the time new, smarter, more
50 expensive chain stores have risen on the new estate, the customers have
vanished. There are undeveloped streets like L— Street used to be, all over
that part of London which planners call 'the decayed inner ring' and which
architects, antiquarians and many others insist must be preserved from the
planners before it is all nibbled away with characterless redevelopment.
55   There is a basic and irreconcilable problem. Survival for the appealing
nineteenth-century fabric of many of the houses has been won in the nick of
time—with a new race of upper-middle-class owners, with a more informed
interest in them. Quite a lot of them will now, probably, be conserved. But the
cost of this in social terms is likely to be a far-reaching change in the nature
60 of the neighbourhood and the contribution it makes towards London. In ten
years from now this change will not yet have fully come to pass, but it might
in twenty. The turn of the century seems likely to see the whole of inner
London parcelled out either into council blocks, with the attendant restrictions and waiting lists, or into highly expensive and inevitably exclusive
65 owner-occupied property. The gain in overall appearance and repair may be
considerable; the loss of opportunities to change one's job without changing
house and in the possibility of living space for those who are neither well-off
nor clever will be immeasurable.

Gillian Tindall, 'A Street in London', *New Society* (1971)

1 Which of the following is nearest in meaning to 'forebodings' as it is used in
line 1 ?

A   Unnecessary worries
B   Vague fears of coming events
C   Constant complaints
D   Strong feelings of disappointment
E   Foolish statements

2 According to the author, people who claim that their street is 'going down' do so for all the following reasons EXCEPT that they are

- **A** afraid of something they cannot reason out
- **B** aware they are growing old themselves
- **C** haunted by some sense of personal inferiority
- **D** uneasy about a feeling they cannot define
- **E** able to recall the days when the houses were new

3 The largely working-class view of London's 'golden age of antiquity' (lines 6–7) included all the following EXCEPT that the

- **A** bingo halls were thriving
- **B** housewives were hardworking
- **C** streets were clean for pedestrians
- **D** gardens were properly looked after
- **E** children were suitably controlled

4 The upper-middle-class view of London was that, up to 1950, most of its

- **A** inhabitants lived in relative comfort
- **B** population lacked all feeling
- **C** entertainment consisted of native dances
- **D** centre was unrelievedly squalid
- **E** streets were full of intelligent children

5 Which of the following is nearest in meaning to 'sober' as it is used in line 12?

- **A** Serious
- **B** Rather downcast
- **C** Courteous
- **D** Well dressed
- **E** Teetotal

6 'A spurious credence is given to' as it is used in line 21 means most nearly the same as

- **A** an unlikely argument is provided for
- **B** a sharp contrast is offered to
- **C** an unusual piece of evidence is suggested for
- **D** a doubtful reinforcement is used for
- **E** an ill-defined explanation is given for

continue overleaf

7 The boom in inner London slum property prices is called 'disproportionate' by the author in line 22 because in 1950 the houses

- **A** were considered valueless
- **B** changed ownership only rarely
- **C** were without gardens
- **D** became eagerly sought after
- **E** were lacking garages

8 According to the article, the boom in inner London property prices was basically due to

- **A** the desire to own a house of one's own
- **B** a fall in the value of money
- **C** the shortage of houses in the country
- **D** a change in upper-middle-class attitudes
- **E** the increased wealth of the working class

9 Features of London streets that have been taken over by the upper middle class are said to include

- 1 window boxes at most of the windows
- 2 no old people to be seen
- 3 lines of expensive cars outside
     no dogs making a mess

- **A** 1 and 2 only
- **B** 1 and 3 only
- **C** 2 and 3 only
- **D** 2 and 4 only
- **E** 3 and 4 only

10 Which of the following is nearest in meaning to 'the social transformation' as it is used in lines 24–5?

- **A** Fluctuation in use and purpose
- **B** New neighbourliness
- **C** Change in status and appearance
- **D** Rapid rebuilding
- **E** Shift in political attitude

11 Features of the houses in L— Street today include all the following features EXCEPT that they

- **A** are roomy
- **B** have gardens
- **C** are close to central London
- **D** have little value
- **E** are over a hundred years old

84

12 The effects of a street becoming 'sought after' (lines 35–6) appear to include all the following EXCEPT that

- **A** local shops and schools are decreasingly used
- **B** there is a growing feeling of belonging to a community
- **C** working-class people move away to other areas
- **D** there is a general improvement in the maintenance of houses
- **E** relatively cheap rooms are no longer available to rent

13 The houses 'benefit' (line 44) from all the following being renewed EXCEPT the

- **A** railings
- **B** tenants
- **C** windows
- **D** owners
- **E** roofs

14 The social advantages which arise from the upper-middle-class's buying up the houses in areas like L— Street include

- 1 working-class people being given alternative council accommodation
- 2 inner London being saved from wholesale destruction and redevelopment
- 3 houses being owned by people with an educated respect for them
- 4 inner London becoming a smart upper-middle-class area

- **A** 1 and 2 only
- **B** 1 and 3 only
- **C** 2 and 3 only
- **D** 2 and 4 only
- **E** 3 and 4 only

15 Those who insist on preserving the old houses of 'the decayed inner ring' (line 52) include

- 1 architects
- 2 students of the past
- 3 working-class tenants
- 4 planners

- **A** 1 and 2 only
- **B** 1 and 3 only
- **C** 2 and 3 only
- **D** 2 and 4 only
- **E** 3 and 4 only

continue overleaf

16 Features of 'the decayed inner ring' (line 52) until recently appear to have included all of the following EXCEPT

- **A** many attractive but run-down rows of houses
- **B** a high proportion of 19th-century houses
- **C** many houses offering rooms to rent
- **D** a high proportion of working-class people
- **E** many small shops being smartened up

17 Which of the following is nearest in meaning to 'parcelled out' as it is used in line 63 ?

- **A** Packed tight
- **B** Organised properly
- **C** Divided up
- **D** Classified deliberately
- **E** Bundled together

18 Changes which the author foresees in the property of inner London by the end of this century include

- 1 a greater level of population density
- 2 only two styles of house architecture
- 3 a better level of property maintenance
- 4 only two very different types of property
- 5 a higher level of smartness

- **A** 1, 2 and 4 only
- **B** 1, 2 and 5 only
- **C** 1, 3 and 4 only
- **D** 2, 3 and 5 only
- **E** 3, 4 and 5 only

19 Two disadvantages of council blocks that the author points out are

- 1 some delays for those requiring accommodation
- 2 limitations on the behaviour of their occupants
- 3 far too many old people living in them
- 4 fewer chances of getting new jobs nearby

- **A** 1 and 2 only
- **B** 1 and 3 only
- **C** 2 and 3 only
- **D** 2 and 4 only
- **E** 3 and 4 only

86

20 According to the article, the 'basic and irreconcilable problem' of inner London (line 55) is that

    A   half its population is rich and selfish and the other half poor and helpless
    B   more cars are owned by people there than there are garages for them
    C   attractive houses are preserved but working-class homes are lost
    D   as some districts become fashionable so others become run-down
    E   money is spent on houses that should be spent on the needs of people

Now go back and check your work

Development

Discussion
Consider whether all houses should belong to the state.
What improvements would you like to see in houses?
Should old houses be preserved?
How can everyone have a good house of his own?

Essays
The demolition men.
The destruction of your neighbourhood.
The deserted house.
What property in your area should be preserved and which should be pulled down and redeveloped? (Give reasons.)
The old home.

Projects
The history of housing.
Where the raw materials for houses come from.
The design of an ideal house.
Housing the homeless.

Activities
Invite a representative of 'Shelter' or the local council to come to introduce a discussion with the class on the subject of local housing problems.
Begin a collection from the local newspapers of interesting items of news about housing developments in your area. Take photographs of buildings you like, houses that are being demolished, new constructions at various states of development so that you can begin a local buildings scrapbook.

As a boy I grew up in the country at a place called Mossbawn in County
Derry. I remember one place in our house that I loved: the top of the dresser.
You had to climb up on a chair and then stand on the lower shelf and peep
over the rim on top. I used to climb up in search of a horseshoe nail to bore a
5   chestnut, or when I wanted the connection for the bicycle pump to pump up a
football, or when I was on the hunt for solution to help me fix a puncture in
my old bicycle. But once I got myself up as far as the top, I forgot what I was
supposed to be looking for and disturbed the dust on a real treasure trove of
stuff that was normally invisible, six feet overhead, beyond the bowls and
10   willow-pattern plates and the eggcups on the top shelf. Old screwdrivers, keys
for the grandfather clock, a small trowel, a broken sharpening stone for the
scythe, pegs rolled with fat coils of string that marked straight lines when you
were digging drills in the garden. Mousetraps, putty gone hard in a screw of
brown paper, a big piece of red rubber cut from a car tube (I always wanted it
15   for the sides of a catapult), hundreds of all sorts of nails. I could have picked
through the cobwebs and musty brown dust for hours but usually someone
caught me.

My father would be out at the fairs and come home with his yellow cane
stick and a smell of cows off his clothes. And maybe he would come in a
20   lorry with three or four bullocks that we'd watch them unload in the yard. The
tripper would come down at the back of the lorry, and the men would climb
up the tall cribs at the side and poke at our cattle to try to turn their heads
down the tripper. Then the other cows and calves in the load would get
excited and start roaring, and then the men would start shouting and my
25   brothers and myself would run and get sticks and stand at gaps and whoop
the cattle to the shed. I'd hear my father say: 'Seamus, you stand at the hen-
house and turn them back. Charlie, you cap them past the pump. You open
the shed door, Pat, and throw a bit of bedding down for them. There's plenty
of straw behind the door. Now boys, get them down that tripper. Hide your
30   sticks. Don't get them excited. That's it. There's one away. Hold back there,
boys, and away she goes again. That's two. Now beat your stick on the cribs
and the big one will work himself down. Come on, you big hallion, you; you're
the best in the bunch. Look at the condition of that beast, boys. Come on; good
man; 'way he goes. Take them easy up the yard now. Pat, you bolt the shed
35   door and throw them a bottle of hay in a minute or two when they settle.
Seamus, run in and tell your mammy to boil a couple of eggs for the lorry

men.' Then when the hubbub had died down and the big lorry reversed and revved itself out of the yard, leaving deep tyre-marks for the rain to collect in, I'd slip down to the shed on my own and look into the dark inside, over the bolted half-door. The cattle would be snoring contentedly, their tails making a gentle swish in the gloom as they munched the hay or chewed the cud.

When I was young I used to go out with an aunt of mine at milking time and if it was wintertime we had a hurricane lamp that was hung up on a bit of wire in the byre. As it swung it sent big soft shadows of the backs of cows swaying and dancing about the rafters and zinc of the roof. I lay snug in a big soft pile of hay, with hayseeds tickling me down the neck of my jersey, smelling the dead summer smells of the hay, listening to the rich purring as the milk rose steadily in my aunt's pail.

In the winter mornings I used to rise and hear the mice scuttling over the ceiling boards; we lived in a thatched house and they must have liked the warm place between the sods and thatch on top and the ceiling-boards below. Then, maybe, I'd go out to the byre again and watch the cows being milked yet another time and if I looked out of the door I could see sparks going up from a neighbour's chimney. One of my neighbours, Joe Ward, was a carpenter and he would be out in his workshop early, starting up his little round stove with big handfuls of dry white woodshavings and cuts of clean timber. He was forever planing shafts for carts, long sides and short rungs for ladders, posts for gates, and planks for rollers. There was a smell of new wood, bright daubs of orange paint on cribs of carts, oily rags to keep implements in good condition.

But we soon had to be on the road to school. Sometimes we could be late. There were water-hens to enjoy on the moss-holes, swimming about with their families among the rushes, and sometimes we happily waited for the big crane to rise, flopping his wide wings. One day we were delighted to see a fox, racing away into the distance like a red ghost. At a certain time it was marbles that held us up; at another time, chestnuts. This is where I learned to be a poet.

I remember a girl who now and again used to come across the fields at night to visit us. As she talked around the fire in our kitchen she would darn holes in any old socks my mother happened to give her. As she talked, the bright needle picked up the stitches and carried the wool, criss-cross, over and under, back and forward, until the hole was miraculously closed over with a crisp web of new wool—and all the time her stories and joking went on and on. I hope I darned my poems as well as she darned those socks, criss-crossing my lines in verses and stitching them up with ideas and rhymes.

Seamus Heaney, 'A Poet's Childhood', *The Listener*

1 Which of the following did the boy NOT find on top of the dresser?

    A   Musty brown dust
    B   Willow-pattern plates
    C   Old screwdrivers
    D   Part of a sharpening stone
    E   Garden lines

2 Whilst the boy was hunting for an object on top of the dresser he invariably

    A   found it
    B   played with it
    C   broke it
    D   looked at it
    E   forgot about it

3 'Drills' (line 13) in this context refer to

    A   deep holes for manure
    B   shallow furrows for seeds
    C   round holes for potatoes
    D   lines for the edges of paths
    E   beds for new flowers

4 Which of the following is nearest in meaning to 'musty' as it is used in line 16?

    A   Stale
    B   Grey
    C   Poisonous
    D   Choking
    E   Cloudy

5 Which of the following is nearest in meaning to 'cribs' as it is used in line 22?

    A   Ladders
    B   Supports
    C   Tarpaulins
    D   Planks
    E   Stalls

6 The 'tripper' (line 23) is a

    A   tail-gate
    B   trolley
    C   cattle-counter
    D   lorry driver
    E   weighing bay

7 All of the following took part in unloading the cattle EXCEPT

    A   Seamus
    B   Charlie
    C   the author's mother
    D   Pat
    E   the author's father

8 The surface of the farm-yard seemed to consist mainly of

    A   soft tarmac
    B   dusty concrete
    C   sharp gravel
    D   slippery mud
    E   hard ruts

9 A 'bottle' of hay (line 35) is a term referring to a

    A   container
    B   bundle
    C   mouthful
    D   hundredweight
    E   load

10 When the cows 'chewed the cud' (line 41) they

    A   swallowed fresh hay
    B   fed whilst asleep
    C   gnawed at their stalls
    D   ate regurgitated food
    E   gulped down straws

11 The shadows swayed and danced about the roof (lines 44–5) because the

    A   aunt moved the light from place to place
    B   cattle shifted about in the shed
    C   wind softly blew the zinc sheets about
    D   boy was playing with the lamp
    E   light was swinging to and fro

12 The 'rich purring' (line 47) was probably caused by the

    A   soft singing of the boy
    B   lowing of the cows
    C   farm cats gathering together
    D   humming of the boy's aunt
    E   milk squirting into the pails

continue overleaf

13 The carpenter seemed to make all of the following EXCEPT

    A sides and steps for ladders
    B bars used for pulling waggons
    C wooden supports for gates
    D flat walls of byres
    E parts of rotating cylinders

14 The 'oily rags' (line 59) were mainly used by the carpenter to

    A lubricate wheels on farmers' carts
    B stop rust from blunting his tools
    C ease nuts that were hard to turn
    D put an edge on his cutting tools
    E polish up the finished woodwork

15 The fact that the boy was sometimes late for school might have been attributed to all the following EXCEPT

    A writing poetry by the roadside
    B watching the pools for signs of life
    C looking for chestnuts on the way
    D observing the wild animals outdoors
    E playing marbles with his friends

16 'Flopping' (line 64) suggests that the flight of the crane was

    A frightening
    B cumbersome
    C powerful
    D hesitant
    E swift

17 The fox is compared with 'a red ghost' (line 65) most probably because he

    A existed only in the boy's imagination
    B could be very malevolent in his actions
    C was very fast-moving and hazy in the distance
    D lacked the normal shape of a fox
    E had been wounded by a farmer and was dying

18 The girl's darning is called 'a crisp web' (lines 72–3) because it is

    A coarse and new
    B woollen and interlaced
    C firm and interwoven
    D quickly and cunningly finished
    E fragile and delicate

19 The girl described in the last paragraph might best be described as

1. an impulsive talker
2. an anxious busy-body
3. a good needle-woman
4. an able servant

A 1 and 2 only
B 1 and 3 only
C 2 and 3 only
D 2 and 4 only
E 3 and 4 only

20 The author says that he found pleasure in all of the following EXCEPT

A cows
B a crane
C mice
D a fox
E water-hens

Now go back and check your work

Development

Further reading
Laurie Lee, *Cider with Rosie*. This is an 'atmospheric' book about a sensitive child's growing-up; new experiences flood in on him; new relationships with people develop; the countryside brings a new awareness to him. This book follows on well from the passage by Seamus Heaney and Dylan Thomas's *Portrait of the Artist as a Young Dog* (see Test One). Gwen Raverat's *Period Piece* gives an account of the childhood of 'a young lady' at the end of the last century; Fred Kitchen's *Brother to the Ox* is a delightful account of a young man's life in the countryside; R. D. Blackmore's classic, *Lorna Doone*, is a romantic, wild story set in the West Country of a young man's love for the daughter of the fierce Doone family.

Discussion
What part does the past play in our present lives? (Is it possible to forget the past? How far are we free to decide our own futures?)

How far does (or should) education detract from (or add to) the richness of the young person's experience?
The advantages of living in the country (or the town).

Written work
Give an account of some incidents from your own early life. (Think about them sensitively and try to recreate the atmosphere of the time as you write.)
Find an old photograph of yourself, family, or friends and tell of the occasion that it captures.
Write about some of the experiences you are having now which one day you are certain you will look back on with fondness and happiness.

Women's expectation of being paid for on every social occasion has always seemed to me to make a mockery of female demands for equal pay.

Once, women rarely had any money of their own. Money was in the hands of their father, husband, son, or any remote male connection rather than in
5 female hands. Even if a woman earned money, it was as likely as not to be handed over to her menfolk. So she had to be paid for.

For many years past, however, the average woman has, at least before marriage, earned her own living. How is it that men are still paying for women—even for equal-pay colleagues? Is it the choice of men? Or of
10 women?

Partly, of course, the custom has survived through habit, partly through embarrassment on both sides about how to reverse it, and partly through approval of the system: it can give a sense of easy security to both participants in the rite. It makes, conventionally, the woman feel properly looked after,
15 and bolsters the man's sense of manliness. Are such play-roles relevant to educated, urban, working people? It's this endless, casual approval of greed that makes it difficult for females to be honest. It's an extension of debilitating childhood conditioning that she'll be looked after when she grows up (i.e. marries). It's getting her into terrible social difficulties. Pre-marriage, she's
20 courted, paid for, has things done for her, just like her penniless, home-bound mother and grandmother. After marriage, not only is there a sudden reversal of the attitudes and activities for which she can expect approval, but she commonly combines her new unfamiliar domestic duties with her full-time job. At least her mother had usually had some practical instruction in
25 cooking and often could expect help with the housework.

It seems to be this rude transition that's causing thousands of indignant women to join Women's Lib. If dowries had been among the conventions which had survived, it would have softened the shock; collecting a dowry would perhaps stem the teenage girl's present appetite for clothes. She often
30 spends every penny she earns on herself and expects boyfriends not only to pay for her entertainment and meals but to acquire a car.

There are countless exceptions to this pattern. Many single women have honest, financially independent relationships with their men, collecting no loot. It's the socially promiscuous woman who wins out; but even for her
35 there's a curious fact—she has to *wait* to be 'asked out'.

continue overleaf

Once parents and family (church and neighbours) arranged a lot of social meetings for the young. Now with more mobility and franker repudiation of the family, it often takes more initiative to get to know people. Increasingly the convention places women in an awkward situation, not only for a few
40 pre-marriage years but (supposing she does marry) for those years after separation or divorce or her husband's death. A single man who feels his life is in the doldrums can do something about it; beginning or continuing relationships is now a male privilege amongst single people. A woman still spends a lot of time simply waiting, isolated by convention.
45 It is surprisingly difficult for a woman to defy this convention. Age helps, but you have to have a great deal of it before it really absolves you. Riches are some assistance. It seems clear that one convention feeds another. Considered in isolation, it's a fatuous convention that rules that a female can't ask a male to go to the theatre or out to dinner. Put it beside the convention
50 that he's the one who's supposed to foot the bill, and it explains itself. Once let it be established that it's polite and pleasant for a woman to take her turn in paying for a man, the relationships between men and women should be a lot calmer and, anyway, viable.
In the meantime it's necessary to be fairly circumspect. Tactics for saving
55 face all round need to be devised. Women in particular have to avoid being over-cheerful or hearty about paying: or, of course, sulky—a female's conditioning has often made her simply *mean*.
It's probably a good idea to foster the habit of separate payment on many occasions (as people often do when eating with someone of the same sex).
60 'Separate bills, please,' is easy enough to say if both parties are willing and if it comes from the woman rather than the man. To ease the change-over women must, if necessary, lie—as they often do now. Useful lies are more available to business women than to others—they can invite someone out to lunch or dinner on the understanding that they'll pay the bill 'on expenses'.
65 But anyone can be 'given' theatre tickets (even if she's going to pay for them) and this is quite a common way, already, for a woman to ask out a male acquaintance or to return his previous hospitality.

J. Alexander, 'Only Two Can Pay',
The Sunday Times Magazine

1 The author suggests that single women make nonsense of their claim for equal pay so long as they

  A   remain unprepared to take the lead in making friendships with men
  B   want men to pay for them when they go out together
  C   take a real pride in being able to earn their own living
  D   are willing to rely on their relatives to support them
  E   show that they cannot cook or run a home on their own

2 Before recent times women were paid for on all social occasions because

    A   money was in short supply for everyone
    B   women enjoyed not having any responsibility
    C   money could be earned only by men
    D   women were not clever enough to control money
    E   money was traditionally in the hands of men

3 According to the article, men still pay for women because people

    1   are used to the social habit
    2   want an excuse to keep women's pay low
    3   approve of the system on the whole
    4   feel indifferent about the whole thing
    5   are embarrassed about altering the situation

    A   1, 2 and 4 only
    B   1, 2 and 5 only
    C   1, 3 and 5 only
    D   2, 3 and 4 only
    E   3, 4 and 5 only

4 According to the article, the advantages of men paying for women are that

    1   most men are encouraged to work harder
    2   both sexes know how the system works
    3   men feel that they are being manly
    4   women can choose whether to go out or not
    5   women feel they are being looked after

    A   1, 2 and 3 only
    B   1, 2 and 5 only
    C   1, 3 and 4 only
    D   2, 3 and 5 only
    E   3, 4 and 5 only

5 Which of the following is nearest in meaning to 'rite' as it is used in line 14?

    A   Ceremony
    B   Custom
    C   Relationship
    D   Obligation
    E   Expense

continue overleaf

6 Which of the following is nearest in meaning to 'debilitating' as it is used in line 17?

    A   Careless
    B   Depressing
    C   Senseless
    D   Enfeebling
    E   Questionable

7 The results of women being paid for by men include all of the following EXCEPT that women

    A   are now meeting serious social problems
    B   become very greedy
    C   build up useful savings before marriage
    D   cannot easily be honest
    E   are encouraged to become over-dependent on men

8 According to the article, all the following are true of modern girls EXCEPT that they usually

    A   can expect men to pay for them before marriage
    B   have better lives than their parents after marriage
    C   have not been taught cookery before marriage
    D   cannot expect help in the home after marriage
    E   have things done for them before marriage

9 One solution that the author offers to help modern girls adjust more easily to marriage is the

    A   reintroduction of the dowry
    B   church as a social institution
    C   help of their parents
    D   Women's Lib. movement
    E   obtaining of a full-time job

10 The article suggests that all the following apply to average teenage girls EXCEPT that they

    A   have an appetite for clothes
    B   spend all their wages on themselves
    C   want to join Women's Lib.
    D   presume men will pay for them
    E   expect their admirers to have a car

11 From the context of the article the 'loot' referred to in line 34 includes all the following items EXCEPT free

- **A** meals
- **B** entertainment
- **C** drinks
- **D** clothes
- **E** travel

12 The 'socially promiscuous' women referred to in line 34 are those who

- **A** calculatedly plan to advance at work by using men
- **B** are immoral in their behaviour with men
- **C** quickly lose the respect of men
- **D** are casual in their treatment of men
- **E** indiscriminately accept hospitality from men

13 According to the article, one social advantage that belongs almost entirely to men is

- **A** owning all the property after marriage
- **B** earning much higher wages than women
- **C** deciding where to live after marriage
- **D** being able to begin relationships with the opposite sex
- **E** having no changes of attitude to make after marriage

14 More enterprise is needed by young people today to meet members of the opposite sex because

- 1 the family is rejected more openly
- 2 people are no longer interested in marriage
- 3 people can move about more easily
- 4 the family has much closer ties

- **A** 1 and 2 only
- **B** 1 and 3 only
- **C** 2 and 3 only
- **D** 2 and 4 only
- **E** 3 and 4 only

15 Which of the following is nearest in meaning to 'in the doldrums' as it is used in line 42 ?

- **A** Sad and lonely
- **B** Full of promise
- **C** Silly and pointless
- **D** Ready to begin
- **E** Dull and static

continue overleaf

16 According to the article, women can take the lead in getting to know men if they are

1   beautiful
2   intelligent in behaviour
3   wealthy
4   no longer young

A   1 and 2 only
B   1 and 3 only
C   2 and 3 only
D   2 and 4 only
E   3 and 4 only

17 Which of the following is nearest in meaning to 'convention' as it is used in line 45?

A   Old-fashioned rule
B   Unnatural way of behaving
C   Generally accepted practice
D   Pompous ceremony
E   Ill-defined attitude

18 According to the article, the two most important things that isolate women in society are that

1   women are not supposed to invite men out
2   men are expected to pay for women's entertainment
3   most women do not earn enough to share expenses
4   most men are too shy to ask women to go out

A   1 and 2 only
B   1 and 3 only
C   2 and 3 only
D   2 and 4 only
E   3 and 4 only

19 Which of the following is nearest in meaning to 'viable' as it is used in line 53?

A   Free from guilt
B   Full of pleasure
C   Easy to manage
D   Capable of discussion
E   Able to flourish

20 Women can avoid embarrassing men when offering to pay at least part of the bill in all of the following ways EXCEPT by

- **A** saying that the expenses will be paid by their firm
- **B** not being too hearty about paying their share
- **C** asking for separate bills by mutual agreement
- **D** insisting that the tradition of men paying is foolish
- **E** implying that they have been given free theatre tickets

Now go back and check your work

Development

Discussion
What faults can you find in the arguments of the passage?
Will men become the inferior sex?
Are girls greedy and men over-privileged in our society?
How far should we allow social conventions to condition our behaviour?

Essays
A good night-out. (You may wish to describe a party, a theatre-visit, or just a social call on friends.)
What qualities do you look for in a future husband (or wife)?
What will Women's Lib. stage demonstrations about in the future?
Some types of boy (or girl) that you dislike. (Try to find reasons for your disapproval.)

Projects
Ancient marriage customs.
Women of international importance (or fame).
Social customs in other parts of the world that are intended to help girls and boys meet each other.

TEST 15

Read the passage and study the tables. Then answer the questions. Do not guess.

Twenty-five per cent of the population actually belong to public libraries, though very often more than one person may be making use of a single ticket. The lowest figure I have come across is that for Leeds, where out of a population of 506,080, covered by 37 separate establishments, there are 84,725 adult
5 borrowers and 18,114 children—i.e. 20·32 per cent of the population (figures for 1968–69). The highest is in Hampstead, where more than 50 per cent of the population belongs: which, if you take into account the ones who can't read yet, and the ones who don't read any more because of failing eyesight, can be reckoned as pretty well saturation.
10 Figures like this would seem to indicate that the 20 per cent of regular library users are not all, or even mostly, drawn from the bookless households. On the contrary. This is borne out by the Plowden report which found that 'a substantially bigger proportion of non-manual than of manual workers' children borrowed from public libraries.'
15 The proportions among children are the important ones, because the library habit is best instilled before the child leaves school. The borough librarian of Camden, W. R. Maidment, puts it like this: 'Where people have left school early, without getting into the habit of reading, we still have something to offer, but persuading adults that there are benefits is hard. We have to con-
20 centrate on the children. Thirty years ago, "Johnny's got his nose in a book" was a term of criticism. Now, with schools having educated a generation of people to library use, it's no longer so. This is the pace we have to go.'
To a large extent, schools are succeeding in this encouragement. In a survey carried out in a comprehensive school in Leeds, among 115 children
25 when they were between the ages of eight and fourteen, 81 did use the public library; 34 did not. But the ones that did tended mostly to come from homes where one would expect to find some books, whereas the non-users were from the non-bookish homes.
Not that libraries are there purely for borrowing books from. When I went
30 to my local library to ask what was available, it turned out that there was an abundance of good things I didn't know about and wasn't using: there are record libraries (though not at my branch), a large central reference library, a collection of historic prints and pictures of the area; and should I wish to do so, I could fill my every evening with the various activities organised by the
35 library service—TV programmes, including all Open University ones every

102

night; film shows (of such films as Buñuel's *Nazarin* and Lotte Lenya in the *Threepenny Opera*), alternating with jazz, folk and poetry recitals, for free, every week; there are chess clubs and talks, and play-readings every Monday. If I were a teacher, I should be welcomed with my class at any of the junior libraries, and my school could borrow a collection of books 'carefully chosen to meet its individual needs' every term, delivered to the door. I could borrow play sets for class play-reading, and illustrations on all aspects of local history for project work. Other library authorities provide art galleries, and small recitals of music.

40

continue overleaf

Table One

The Ownership of Books and Library Membership

Group	Number of books owned	% of those in the group who are library members	% of those who belong to the library who are members of the group
1	none	6	2
2	1–20	15	17
3	21–50	25	24·5
4	51–100	31	24·5
5	101–200	37	16
6	over 200	52	16

Table Two

Sex, Age, Class, Education and Library Membership

Group	% of those in the group who are library members	% of those who belong to the library who are members of the group
sex		
Male	27	50
Female	22·5	50
age		
15–19	45	12
20–34	27	28
35–54	20	31
55–64	24	14
65 or more	23	14
not given	–	1
class		
Professional	44	20
Managerial	42	28
Skilled manual	16	16
Semi-skilled manual	10	9
Unskilled manual	8	3
Others	–	24
education		
University/equivalent	74	17
Technical/commercial college	32	11
Grammar/public school	45	34
Secondary modern school	14	37
Others	25	1

Table Three

School (or Higher Education) Leaving Age, Intelligence,
Newspaper (and Magazine) Readers and Library Membership

Group	% of those in the group who are library members	% of those who belong to the library who are members of the group
school (or higher education) leaving age		
Under 15	14	26
15	14	14
16–18	40	35
19 or more	56	15
Still in education	62	10
intelligence		
Top 10% (decile)	62	34
2nd decile	31	17
3rd decile	27	8
4th decile	23	7
5th decile	27	8
6th decile	12	5
7th decile	15	4
8th decile	12	2
9th decile	19	8
Bottom 10% (decile)	15	7
newspaper (and magazine) readers		
Those taking a national Sunday paper	26	96
Those taking a national daily paper	26	94
Those taking any magazine	28	55
Those taking a local daily/evening newspaper	30	51
Those taking a local weekly paper	32	74

(based on) Ruth Brandon, 'The Library's Public', *New Society*

1 The percentage of the population which makes use of a public library is likely to be

- **A** 20%
- **B** 25%
- **C** 20–25%
- **D** less than 20%
- **E** more than 25%

2 The highest percentages of children who use the library come from homes where there are

- 1 no books
- 2 non-reading parents
- 3 some books
- 4 non-manual workers

- **A** 1 and 2 only
- **B** 1 and 3 only
- **C** 2 and 3 only
- **D** 2 and 4 only
- **E** 3 and 4 only

3 Which of the following is nearest in meaning to 'instilled' as it is used in line 16?

- **A** Shared by the teacher at school
- **B** Dropped gradually into the mind
- **C** Suggested repeatedly by adults
- **D** Introduced into routine work
- **E** Encouraged by firm example

4 It is easier to persuade children to use the public library than adults because the children are more

- **A** ready to adopt the habit
- **B** educated than earlier generations
- **C** restricted in their choice
- **D** anxious to find information
- **E** able to profit from reading

5 It is difficult to persuade adults that there are benefits in using the public library probably because they are, in general,

- **A** without any education
- **B** set in their ways
- **C** too busy to read
- **D** not able to concentrate
- **E** trained for manual work

106

6 The passage suggests that schools have been responsible for

   A making children read too much
   B dividing children and parents
   C changing the pace of life
   D showing children how to use libraries
   E turning the young into intellectual snobs

7 From the survey carried out in a comprehensive school in Leeds (lines 23–8) one can reasonably conclude that

   A children there enter comprehensive schools at the age of eight
   B Leeds schools have a wider range of children than those elsewhere
   C home environment affects the use made of the library
   D the majority of children surveyed came from non-bookish homes
   E schools in Leeds concentrate most on children's reading skills

8 Which of the following is nearest in meaning to 'abundance' as it is used in line 31 ?

   A Supply
   B Profusion
   C Excess
   D Selection
   E Harvest

9 A 'reference library' (line 32) contains books which

   A can be consulted but not removed
   B are stored for future use only
   C have a very restricted value
   D are available to all for borrowing
   E may only be used by serious students

10 Which of the following is nearest in meaning to 'prints' as it is used in line 33 ?

   A Paintings
   B Drawings
   C Reproductions
   D Photocopies
   E Portraits

continue overleaf

11 According to the passage all of the following are available through the writer's public library service EXCEPT

    A   records for borrowing
    B   educational TV programmes
    C   musical and literary entertainment
    D   theatrical productions
    E   lectures and games

12 Public libraries help schools by providing all of the following EXCEPT

    A   sets of books for class use
    B   opportunities for visits by school parties
    C   book-lending services
    D   study-pictures of their areas
    E   drama and pop festivals

13 'Project work' (line 43) can be all of the following EXCEPT work that is

    A   based on a central theme
    B   finished in pupils' own time
    C   carried out by team effort
    D   followed up because of its interest
    E   intended only for slow pupils

14 Table One suggests all of the following EXCEPT

    A   31 % of those owning between 51 and 100 books belong to the library
    B   16% of library members own more than 200 books
    C   16% of those owning between 101 and 200 books belong to the library
    D   17% of library members own between 1 and 20 books
    E   52% of those owning more than 200 books belong to the library

15 Which of the following statements CANNOT be supported from the tables?

    A   20% of those who are in the 35–54 age group belong to the library
    B   The percentage of men belonging to the library is greater than that of women
    C   Just over a quarter of those in the 20–34 age group belong to the library
    D   There is a tendency for people to use the library more as they grow older
    E   Nearly half of those who are in their late teens belong to the library

16 According to the tables which of the following is MOST likely to be a member of the library?

    A   A doctor
    B   An apprentice
    C   A sales manager
    D   An export director
    E   A factory foreman

17 Which of the following statements CAN be supported from Table Two?

    A Middle-aged people form the majority of library members
    B The more skilled a manual worker is the more likely he will be to join the library
    C Education makes very little difference to a person's use of the library
    D The lowest proportion of those belonging to the library is found amongst teenagers
    E Libraries are a powerful factor in encouraging differences between the classes

18 Which of the following statements CAN be supported from Table Three?

    A 34% of library members belong to the most intelligent group
    B Those who are still in education form the majority of library members
    C 7% of the least intelligent group belong to the library
    D Library membership decreases constantly in proportion to the decrease in intelligence
    E 40% of library members are persons who left school between sixteen and eighteen

19 Which TWO of the following statements can be deduced from Table Three?

    1 Nearly all who belong to the library take a local daily paper
    2 Just over a quarter of those taking a national daily paper belong to the library
    3 About half of those who take a magazine also belong to the library
    4 Most of those who belong to the library also take a national Sunday paper

    A 1 and 2 only
    B 1 and 3 only
    C 2 and 3 only
    D 2 and 4 only
    E 3 and 4 only

20 From the tables all of the following statements can be deduced EXCEPT

    A The more books a person owns the more likely he is to belong to the library
    B University graduates are the most likely group to form the majority of library members
    C The time when a person is the most likely to be a member of the library is during his teens
    D Women are less likely to be members of the library than men
    E The less skilled a person is the less likely he is to belong to the library

Now go back and check your work

109

Development

Discussion

Invite the school librarian to talk about the library in your own community. He might be asked to suggest or recommend some of the material in it which you would find interesting (e.g. the careers section).

Are libraries fair to authors? (Some writers complain that extensive use of libraries cuts down their income from sales; but public libraries can help writers, too.)

What social services ought to be provided out of the rates?

Written work

Write a review of a library book you have read (and liked) recently.

What do you think are the main contributions that a school library should make to the life of the school?

Projects

Pay a visit to your public library to build up a report on all its services. Some of the services which libraries offer are mentioned in the article; does your library offer more? Find out what it likes to specialise in. How are books purchased? Who decides which books to buy? How are they prepared for issue? How many books are lost? What more would the librarian like to do if he had more money to spend?

You may like to attempt a survey of library-use (public or school library) within your own school or college. (Decide what facts you would like to find out; devise the right, clear questions you should ask; make sure your 'sampling' is fair. If you decide to use a questionnaire you should consult a member of the staff who has had experience of constructing one—they are not easy to work out!)

We had not been long at sea before the first shark visited us. And sharks soon became an almost daily occurrence. Sometimes the shark just came swimming up to inspect the raft and went on in search of prey after circling round us once or twice. But most often the sharks took up a position in our wake
5 just behind the steering oar, and there they lay without a sound, stealing from starboard to port and very occasionally giving a leisurely wag of their tails to keep pace with the raft's placid advance. The blue-grey body of the shark always looked brownish in the sunlight just below the surface, and it moved up and down with the seas so that the dorsal fin always stuck up menacingly.
10 If there was a high sea the shark might be lifted up by the waves above our own level, and we had a direct side view of the shark as in a glass case, as it swam towards us in a dignified manner with its fussy retinue of small pilot fish ahead of its jaws. For a few seconds it looked as if both the shark and its striped companions would swim right on board, till the raft leant over grace-
15 fully to leeward, rose over the ridge of the waves and descended on the other side.

To begin with we had a great respect for sharks on account of their repu-tation and their alarming appearance. There was an unbridled strength in the streamlined body, consisting just of one great bundle of steel muscles, and a
20 heartless greed in the broad flat head with the small cat's eyes and the enor-mous jaws which could swallow footballs. When the man at the helm shouted, 'Shark alongside to starboard' or 'Shark alongside to port' we used to come out in search of hand harpoons and gaffs and station ourselves along the edge of the raft. The shark usually glided round us regally with the dorsal
25 fin close up to the logs. Our respect for the shark increased when we saw that the gaffs bent like spaghetti when we struck them against the sandpaper armour on the shark's back, while the spearheads of the hand harpoons were broken in the heat of the battle. All we gained by getting through the shark's skin and into the gristle or muscles was a hectic struggle, in which the water
30 boiled round us till the shark broke loose and was off, while a little oil floated up and spread itself over the surface.

To save our last harpoon head we fastened together a bunch of our largest fish-hooks and hid them inside the carcase of a whole dolphin. We slung the bait overboard with a precautionary multiplication of steel lines fastened to a
35 piece of our own lifeline. Slowly and surely the shark came, and as it lifted its
continue overleaf

snout above the water it opened its great crescent-shaped jaws with a jerk and let the whole dolphin slip in and down. There it stuck. There was a struggle in which the shark lashed the water into foam, but we had a good grip of the rope and hauled the big fellow, despite his resistance, as far as the logs aft,
40 where he lay awaiting what might come and gaped as though to intimidate us with his parallel rows of saw-like teeth. Here we profited by a sea to slide the shark up over the low end logs, slippery with seaweed, and after casting a rope round the tail fin we ran well out of the way till the war dance was over.

Thor Heyerdahl, The Kon-Tiki Expedition

1 Where did the sharks near the raft most often position themselves?

    A In front
    B Behind
    C To the right
    D Beneath
    E To the left

2 'Placid advance' (line 7) suggests that the craft was moving forward

    A noiselessly
    B slowly
    C relentlessly
    D unevenly
    E pleasingly

3 The dorsal fins of the following sharks always remained above the surface of the water because the sharks

    A rose and fell with the movement of the waves
    B were threatening the raft, thinking it to be a fish
    C moved alternately from starboard to port of the raft
    D used them to maintain balance and sense direction
    E intended to frighten the men by their display

4 One of the sharks seemed to be 'in a glass case' (line 11) because

    A it was about to be killed as a specimen
    B the side of the raft was made of strong glass
    C it was being viewed through the raft's planks
    D the shark seemed lifeless to all who saw it
    E it seemed to be fixed in a transparent container

5 The small pilot fish are described as 'fussy' (line 12) because they

    A   were coloured with bright, lively spots
    B   proved difficult about what they would eat
    C   were attentive to the shark's every movement
    D   worked out carefully which path to take
    E   were small compared with the shark's size

6 The shark's companions described as 'striped' (line 14) were the

    A   tiger sharks swimming nearby
    B   waves streaked by sunlight
    C   pilot fish swimming ahead
    D   shiny, blue-grey sharks
    E   oil-streaked pieces of débris

7 It seemed at one moment that the shark would 'swim right on board' (line 14) because

    A   it was leaping high from the water and dropping again
    B   the raft almost overturned in the high seas
    C   it was making an aggressive run against the raft
    D   the raft was below the wave containing the shark
    E   it managed to get its jaws on board at one time

8 The strength of the shark's body is described as 'unbridled' (line 18) because it was

    A   horse-like
    B   misdirected
    C   uncontrollable
    D   enormous
    E   unused

9 All the characteristics of the shark mentioned seem appropriate to its size and power EXCEPT its

    A   muscles
    B   head
    C   dorsal fin
    D   jaws
    E   eyes

10 The helmsman's position on the raft was

    A   forward
    B   on the starboard
    C   amidships
    D   on the port
    E   at the rear

continue overleaf

11 The shark's way of swimming as it approached the raft seemed, from the author's description, to be very

    A determined
    B angry
    C aggressive
    D stately
    E listless

12 The sailors' admiration of the sharks increased owing to the sharks'

    A frightening appearance
    B ugly reputations
    C steel muscles
    D hard backs
    E piercing eyes

13 Which of the following is nearest in meaning to 'gaffs' as it is used in line 23?

    A Barbed fishing-spears
    B Strong, curved oars
    C Long, thin harpoons
    D Heavy steel jemmies
    E Sharp steering-blades

14 The comparison 'like spaghetti' (line 26) is introduced mainly to suggest that the gaffs were

    A thin
    B white
    C brittle
    D long
    E soft

15 The struggle between the men and the fish is described as 'hectic' (line 29) because it

    A was uneven
    B lasted a long time
    C was frenzied
    D produced no definite results
    E was cruel

16 'A precautionary multiplication of steel lines' (line 34) suggests that the sailors

    A decided to send out more than one decoy
    B increased the number of lines to avoid losing their prey
    C interwove many lines in order to match the shark's strength
    D lengthened the lines to keep the sharks at a distance
    E tested the strength of the lines again and again

17 Which of the following is nearest in meaning to 'intimidate' as it is used in line 40?

   A Inform
   B Excite
   C Warn
   D Frighten
   E Impress

18 'We profited by a sea' (line 41) suggests that the shark was hauled aboard when the sea

   A was calm and still for a moment
   B broke over the end of the raft
   C gave up its victim in the end
   D lifted the raft clear of the waves
   E made the raft glide forward quickly

19 'War dance' (line 43) indicates that in dying the shark had

   A cried out menacingly
   B tied itself up
   C attacked the men
   D moved in a circle
   E threshed about wildly

20 Until one was finally captured, the sharks had

   A attacked the raft fearlessly
   B swallowed everything thrown away
   C broken free from the fishing lines
   D tried to swim on board the raft
   E attempted to tip the craft over

Now go back and check your work

Development

Further reading

E. Hemingway, *The Old Man and the Sea*—another interesting account of the struggles of man with the sea and its creatures which try to destroy his hopes and dreams. Nicholas Monsarrat's *The Cruel Sea* tells of the fight of seamen during the last war, not only with the enemy but with the fierceness of the sea itself.

Discussion
What rights does a country have over the waters round its coasts? (Oil, sea-pollution, fishing, defence are some of the topics you may wish to discuss.) What opportunities are there for young men or women to make a career at sea today? (The Royal Navy, the Merchant Service and the Royal National Lifeboat Institution will be able to help you with information, films, literature and possibly visiting speakers.)

Essays
Tell the story of an adventure you have had on the sea.
The debt the nation owes to the sea. (You may use any relevant geographical, historical or scientific knowledge you have here.)

Projects
Undersea exploration.
The adventures of a great explorer.
The richness of the sea.
Ancient boat-building (e.g. Egyptian, Viking, Roman).

If the Road Research Laboratory's professional crystal-gazers are proved
right there will be 34,200,000 vehicles—including 29,100,000 cars—on our
roads by the year 2000, enough, in other words, to create a nose-to-tail jam
about 97,000 miles long. We shall be near the saturation figure of one car for
5   every two people—men, women and children—and future increases will tend
to run in harness with population growth.

Nelson Mills Baldwin, the recently appointed Secretary-General of the
Royal Automobile Club, was asked to study his crystal ball:

'In the opinion of the RAC, this problem of rapidly increasing numbers of
10   motor vehicles in our towns will not be solved by negative restrictions such
as parking meters, which are only a means of extorting more money from the
motorist and contribute nothing towards solving the problem. Our Technical
and Engineering Committee forecast some time ago that the day might come
when ordinary cars would be left on the outskirts of cities and specially-
15   designed runabouts used within the city itself. Meanwhile, the only short-
term answer is adequate off-street parking at a reasonable price, combined
with inner and outer ring roads and pedestrian precincts. That way, com-
muters, shoppers, visitors, business people—afoot or awheel—can all be
reasonably happy.'

20   Alec Durie, Director-General of the Automobile Association, isn't worried
by the thought of over 34 million vehicles on roads within thirty years:

'Progress means a motorway network of three thousand miles completed
by 1980, and speedy and imaginative development of a city route system.
Experience all over the world shows that the construction of city motorways
25   is fundamental to our environment. Alongside an increasing vehicle population, tourism will grow as a No. 1 industry, as more free time becomes
available to the average family and motorways shorten travelling time between
cities and leisure areas. It is essential, therefore, that serious and constructive
thought is given to catering for vehicles at their destination. Parking accom-
30   modation, already a problem in our towns, must be high on the list of
priorities as must be, for instance, the development of caravan and camping
sites.'

Unfortunately, Britain has not been building motorways at a notably brisk
rate. The first section—the M6's by-pass of Preston—was opened in 1958,
35   but the thousandth mile was not due for completion until 1972. In contrast,
continue overleaf

West Germany expected to have 4,000 motorway miles open by then. Italy's figure was 3,300 and the French talked confidently in terms of 1,500. The rate of motorway growth planned for West Germany and France in the next ten years is about three times greater than our own.

40 If roadbuilding cannot keep pace with the increase in motor vehicles, what hope is there of motoring being anything but a dismal chore in the years ahead? The driver prepared to use a map, plan a journey and make use of the world's best network of secondary roads should be able to motor around Britain in relative sanity for many years to come. Driving regularly between

45 London and Shropshire I carefully avoid both the M1 and the A5 and, for the sake of an extra fifteen-or-so minutes' travelling time, can enjoy some of England's most beautiful countryside.

We may also see the growth of schemes in cities which, although closing roads to private vehicles at certain times, provide acceptable alternatives. A

50 pioneering experiment along these lines has been operating in the Peak District National Park. Visitors to the beautiful Goyt Valley pay to park and are then transported, free of charge, by mini-buses. Footpaths, picnic places, informative leaflets and a nature trail are provided.

Another point is that alternative forms of private transport may become

55 widely available by the year 2000. The current rate of technological progress does not preclude the possibility of 'family helicopters'—or similar devices— being on the market at a reasonable price by the end of the century. Moving pavements—a luxury only enjoyed at certain airports at the moment—may join forces with dial-a-destination taxi services to revolutionise transport.

P. Llewellyn, 'How many cars can Britain take?'
The Sunday Times Magazine

1 The Road Research Laboratory assumed that by the year 2000 Great Britain's population will be about

    A 58,200,000
    B 65,500,000
    C 68,400,000
    D 75,750,000
    E 88,100,000

2 Which of the following is nearest in meaning to 'run in harness with' as it is used in line 6?

    A Counteract the problem of
    B Keep pace with
    C Diminish the importance of
    D Move directly against
    E Reflect the development of

3 When Nelson Mills Baldwin was asked to study his crystal ball (line 8) he was really being asked to

    A   produce clear reports
    B   put his trust in luck
    C   look into the future
    D   examine all the possibilities
    E   guess the best plan of action

4 Parking meters were said to be 'negative restrictions' (line 10) because they

    A   were the only way of dealing effectively with the car in the city
    B   were disliked intensely by many motorists without the necessary change
    C   had never been given official approval by many motoring organisations
    D   collected money from the motorist but did not help solve traffic congestion
    E   hindered the solution of the questions posed by the motor car in towns

5 The Royal Automobile Club's short-term answers to the problem of the car in the city included all of the following EXCEPT

    A   sufficient off-street parking
    B   pedestrian precincts
    C   inner and outer ring roads
    D   reasonably priced parking
    E   well laid-out roundabouts

6 The spokesmen for the Royal Automobile Club and the Automobile Association agreed that more thought must be given to

    A   parking
    B   pedestrian precincts
    C   tourism
    D   caravan sites
    E   motorways

7 The Automobile Association's solution to Britain's car problems included all of the following EXCEPT

    A   a city route system
    B   the expansion of caravan and camping sites
    C   adequate parking space
    D   the closing of roads permanently to vehicles
    E   a motorway network

continue overleaf

8 Which of the following is nearest in meaning to 'pedestrian precincts' as it is used in line 17?

   A   Roads where vehicles are limited to certain hours
   B   Areas where people on foot only are allowed to go
   C   Parks for children and old people to use
   D   Areas reserved for those who have no cars of their own
   E   Streets reserved for children to play games

9 Which of the following is nearest in meaning to 'environment' as it is used in line 25?

   A   Economy
   B   Housing
   C   Travel
   D   Surroundings
   E   Pleasure

10 Alec Durie argued (lines 22–32) that progress included all of the following EXCEPT

   A   an increase in tourism
   B   the development of city routes
   C   a planned increase in car numbers
   D   shorter time to complete journeys
   E   an increase in leisure time

11 Germany's rate of motorway-building since 1958, compared with Britain's, was

   A   twice as slow
   B   about the same
   C   half as fast
   D   marginally better
   E   four times faster

12 According to the author, ways of preventing car journeys in Britain from becoming 'a dismal chore' (line 41) included all the following EXCEPT

   A   using a map
   B   planning the journey
   C   using secondary roads
   D   stopping to enjoy the countryside
   E   avoiding the motorways

13 According to the article, Britain had the world's finest

A system of secondary roads
B scenery
C methods of tackling car problems
D motorways
E ideas for future vehicles

14 The author made his journey from London to Shropshire more bearable by

A never wasting his time by stopping on the way
B travelling as directly as possible
C losing some time in exchange for seeing fine countryside
D getting to know the road well by regularly using it
E consulting the Automobile Association before starting

15 A 'pioneering experiment' as it is used in line 50 is an experiment which is

A the easiest to conduct
B crude and primitive
C the first to succeed
D unreliable and unsuccessful
E the earliest to be tried

16 Features provided in the Goyt Valley experiment included all the following EXCEPT

A footpaths
B parking space
C natural tracks
D free mini-buses
E information leaflets

17 'Technological progress' as it is used in line 55 is essentially progress which depends on

A military developments
B scientific advances
C educational reforms
D sociological advances
E atomic experiments

18 Which of the following is nearest in meaning to 'join forces with' as it is used in line 59?

A Attack
B Lead to
C Replace
D Compete with
E Complement

continue overleaf

19 Ideas in the article for easing the problems of the car in the city in the future included all the following EXCEPT

A   roads where vehicles are banned
B   free public transport
C   private air transport
D   travelling pavements
E   driverless automatic taxis

20 Forms of transport foreseen in the cities of the future included all the following EXCEPT

A   specially-designed runabouts
B   luxury buses
C   dial-a-destination taxis
D   moving pavements
E   private helicopters

Now go back and check your work

Development

Discussion
Will the car destroy the city?
How can cars (or motor-cycles) be improved (*a*) to stop accidents, and (*b*) to reduce pollution?
Why are cars designed as they are?

Written Work
Suggest some ways in which cars and the environment can be brought into a harmonious relationship.
The car rally.
If you were made the Minister of Transport with unlimited powers what would be your first FOUR Acts of Parliament? (Discuss your reasons fully.)
The city of the future.

Projects
The history of the car.
Some famous cars.
Veteran cars.
Famous women car drivers.
The world's supply of oil.

122

Activities

Make a survey of the road traffic at an important place in your area (e.g where a pedestrian crossing is needed; where traffic jams occur regularly; where accidents take place. The local police may be able to help you select a suitable site.) Decide what facts you wish to find out and then draw up a simple but clear data sheet. You may be able to publish your findings in the school magazine.

TEST 18

Read the passage. Then answer the questions. Do not guess.

When Michael reached the gate of Randell House, he longed to turn back with his mother.

'Don't come in with me,' he whispered. 'And don't wave, will you?' he begged. Then with an effort he joined the stream of boys walking confidently
5 through the big gate.

In the entrance hall a ginger-haired foxy-faced man in a green uniform said sharply:

'New boy?'

Michael nodded.
10 'Stand on one side, please. The Headmaster will see you presently.'

Michael waited. He noticed with pride that the boy next to him had brought with him either his mother or his sister. Michael felt very superior.

The preliminaries of Michael's career at Randell House passed in a dream-like confusion of thought and action. First of all he waited anxiously in the
15 Headmaster's study in an atmosphere of morocco-leather and large waste-paper baskets, and as in every other room in which Michael had waited, whether of dentist or doctor, the outlook from the window was gloomy. He was glad when Mr Randell led him and several other boys towards the First Form, where in a dream peopled by the swinging legs of many boys, he learnt
20 from a scarlet book.

At eleven o'clock a bell throbbed through the school, and Michael, before he knew what was happening, was carried in a torrent of boys towards the playground. Michael had never felt supreme loneliness, even at night, until he stood in the middle of that green prairie of recreation distinguishing nobody,
25 a very small creature in a throng of chattering giants. Some of these giants approached him.

'Hullo, are you a new kid?'

Michael breathed his 'yes'.

'What's your first name?'
30 This was a terribly direct attack, and Michael was wondering whether it would be best to run quickly out of the playground, to keep silence or to surrender the information, when the quick and authoritative voice of Rodber flashed from behind him.

'Fish and find out, young Biden.'
35 'Who are you calling young, young Rodber?'

'You,' said Rodber. 'So you'd better scoot off and leave this kid alone.'

124

'Church said I was to collar all the new boys for his gang,' Biden explained.

'Did he? Well, this one's in our gang, so there!'

'Look here,' said Rodber presently, 'you'd better come and see Pearson.
40 He's the oldest boy in school and the captain of our gang and for goodness'
sake look a bit cheerful.'

Michael forced a grin such as photographers conjure.

Under the shade of a gigantic tree stood Pearson, the leader, languidly
eating a very small and very unripe pear.
45 'Hello, Pinky,' he drawled.

'Hello, Pearson,' said Rodber in a reverent voice, 'I know this kid at home.
He's keen to be allowed to join your gang.'

Pearson scarcely glanced at Michael.

'All right. Swear him in. I've got a new oath written down in a book at
50 home, but he can take the old one.'

After this Michael felt in a somewhat elated frame of mind, and when he
returned to the school yard, he felt bold enough to watch a game of conkers.
Michael was amazed when one of the two solemn-faced antagonists suddenly grabbed his new school-cap and put it in his pocket and, without paying
55 any attention to him, went on with his conkers as if nothing had happened.
Michael had no idea how to grapple with the situation and felt inclined to
cry.

'I say, give me my cap,' he said at last.

The solemn-faced boys went on in silence with the game.
60 'Please give me my cap,' Michael asked again.

No notice was taken of his appeal and Michael, looking round in despair,
saw Rodber. He ran up to him.

'Rodber, that boy over there has got my cap,' he said.

'Well, don't come sneaking to me. Go and hit him,' said Rodber.
65 'Really?' asked Michael.

'Of course.'

Michael was not prepared to withstand Rodber's advice, so he went up to
the solemn-faced boy and hit him as hard as he could. The solemn-faced boy
was so much surprised by this attack that he did not for a moment retaliate,
70 and it was only his friend's gasp 'What cheek', that restored him to a sense
of what had happened.

In a moment Michael found himself lying on his back and almost smothered
by the solemn-faced boy's whole body and presently suffering agony from the
pressure of the solemn-faced boy's knees upon his arms pinioned crosswise.
75 Excited voices chattered about him from an increasing circle. He heard the
solemn-faced boy telling his horrified auditors that a new boy had hit him.
He heard various punishments strongly recommended, and at last with a
sense of relief he heard the quick authoritative voice of the ubiquitous
Rodber.
80 'Let him up, young Plummer. A fight! A fight!'

continue overleaf

Plummer got up, as he was told, and Michael in a circle of eager faces found himself confronted by Plummer.

'Go on,' shouted Rodber. 'I'm backing you, young Fane.'

Michael lowered his head and charged desperately forward for the honour
85 of Rodber; but a terrible punch on his nose and another on his arm and a third on his chin brought tears and blood together in such quantity that Michael would have liked to throw himself on to the grass and weep his life out, too weak to contend with solemn-faced boys who snatched caps.

Then over his misery he heard Rodber cry, 'That's enough. It's not fair.
90 Give him back his cap.' The crowd broke up except for a few admirers of Rodber, who was telling Michael that he had done tolerably well for a new boy.

C. Mackenzie, Sinister Street

1 Michael did not want his mother to accompany him into Randell House because he

- **A** wanted to behave like the other boys
- **B** was ashamed of his mother's appearance
- **C** feared that other boys would jeer at him
- **D** knew she would not wait patiently for the Head
- **E** thought that women were not allowed to enter

2 'With an effort' (line 4) implies that Michael was

- **A** carrying a load of books
- **B** lazy
- **C** finding his new uniform awkward
- **D** lame
- **E** unsure of himself

3 'The stream of boys' (line 4) suggests most strongly that the boys were moving

- 1 noisily and excitedly
- 2 in some kind of line
- 3 in a disorganised manner
- 4 at a regular pace

- **A** 1 and 2 only
- **B** 1 and 3 only
- **C** 2 and 3 only
- **D** 2 and 4 only
- **E** 3 and 4 only

4 'Foxy-faced' (line 6) implies that the man's facial features were

1 sinister
2 sharp
3 cruel
4 crafty

A 1 and 2 only
B 1 and 3 only
C 2 and 3 only
D 2 and 4 only
E 3 and 4 only

5 During his first morning at Randell House Michael did all of the following EXCEPT

A go to see his Headmaster
B study a book
C feel very lonely
D join Pearson's gang
E win a fight

6 'Dream-like' (lines 13–14) and 'dream' (line 19) are used in the description of Michael's first morning at Randell House because he

A missed his mother subconsciously
B was not yet wide awake
C felt so small when everything else was huge
D was experiencing strange events and feelings
E found being at school was a nightmare

7 At break the boys moved towards the playground as if they were a mass of fast-moving

A rocks
B water
C clouds
D fire
E lava

8 In common with dentists' and doctors' waiting-rooms the Headmaster's study is said to have had

A a dream-like quality
B morocco-leather upholstery
C a nervous group of occupants
D waste-paper baskets
E a depressing view outside

continue overleaf

9 'Throbbed' (line 21) implies that the bell's major quality was its

  A   harshness
  B   echo
  C   pulsation
  D   shrillness
  E   duration

10 'Prairie' (line 24) is used to describe the recreation area as it appeared to Michael probably because it seemed

  1   large
  2   empty
  3   flat
  4   grassy
  5   hard

  A   1, 2 and 3 only
  B   1, 2 and 5 only
  C   1, 3 and 4 only
  D   2, 4 and 5 only
  E   3, 4 and 5 only

11 Michael was unwilling to give his first name (lines 30–2) because he probably felt that Biden's approach had

  A   put him in great difficulty with the other boys
  B   stopped him from remaining merely one of the crowd
  C   destroyed any chance he had of choosing his own gang
  D   been much too pointed and personal
  E   placed him in the boy's power in some magical way

12 Which of the following is nearest in meaning to 'authoritative' as it is used in line 32?

  A   Commanding
  B   Frightening
  C   Grating
  D   Insistent
  E   Snarling

13 From the conversation between Rodber and Biden (lines 34–8) it seems that Biden was probably about the same age as

  A   Michael
  B   Pearson
  C   Rodber
  D   Church
  E   Plummer

128

14 Joining Pearson's gang appears to have involved all of the following EXCEPT

- **A** being selected
- **B** passing a test
- **C** being accepted
- **D** meeting the leader
- **E** taking an oath

15 The boy who snatched Michael's cap was

- **A** Biden
- **B** Plummer
- **C** Church
- **D** Pearson
- **E** Rodber

16 'Such as photographers conjure' (line 42) is used to describe Michael's **grin** probably because it was

- 1 insincere
- 2 normal
- 3 exaggerated
- 4 spontaneous

- **A** 1 and 2 only
- **B** 1 and 3 only
- **C** 2 and 3 only
- **D** 2 and 4 only
- **E** 3 and 4 only

17 'Pinioned crosswise' (line 74) is best explained as

- **A** held fast as if extended for a crucifixion
- **B** bound tightly at the wrist with a cord
- **C** stretched tightly well above his head
- **D** pinned down close to the shoulders
- **E** crushed sideways below his body

18 During his first morning at school Michael experienced all of the following EXCEPT feelings of

- **A** superiority
- **B** loneliness
- **C** boredom
- **D** uncertainty
- **E** misery

continue overleaf

19 Randell House appears to have had all of the following EXCEPT

    A   a main gate
    B   an entrance hall
    C   a headmaster's study
    D   a grass-covered playground
    E   an assembly hall

20 All of the following appear to be true of Michael EXCEPT that he was

    A   surnamed Fane
    B   willing to conform
    C   in the First Form
    D   acceptable to Pearson
    E   insensitive to pain

Now go back and check your work

Development

Discussion
What are the causes of bullying? How can they be removed?
Should schools be organised in traditional ways (forms, houses, prefects, housemasters, etc.)?
Why are children so sensitive and adults so insensitive?
Should one be able to buy a better education for one's children?

Written work
Your first day in new surroundings.
School games and pastimes of which parents do not approve.
The big fight.

Projects
The School's history.
The story of school uniform and its development.
The noble art of boxing.

TEST 19 *Read the passage. Then answer the questions. Do not guess.*

17,000 babies were born in the week March 3–9, 1958. The National Children's Bureau managed to mount a study on the home background, health, and physical and mental development of the children at seven.

Are some children more equal than others?

5 The chances of an unskilled manual worker's child being a poor reader at seven years old are six times greater than those of a middle-class child. One explanation for this is the home background of most middle-class children; they arrive at school tuned in not only to the educational demands but also to the way they are expected to behave in school. The early difficulties of
10 some working-class children in adapting themselves sometimes result in alienation. Our results show that more working-class children, even by seven years of age, are showing hostility towards teachers or, worse still, withdrawal, depression and a 'writing-off' of adult standards.

What effect does housing have on reading?

15 We compared the attainment and adjustment of children whose families had the sole use of hot water, indoor lavatory and bathroom with those whose families had not. The 'haves' were on average nine months ahead in reading. The 'have-nots' were also behind in arithmetic and were less well adjusted in school. Obviously you can't put in a bath and expect an immediate improve-
20 ment in a child's reading. Yet bad housing conditions can lead to poor health, depression and irritability in parents and children; they may also produce a feeling of alienation from the more privileged sector of society (with which the school may be identified).

Is a big family ideal?

25 Not in terms of attainment and adjustment at school. A seven-year-old from a one- or two-child family is on average about twelve months advanced in reading compared with one from a family of five or more. He is also likely to be three months ahead in arithmetic, better adjusted in school and rather taller. A large family's resources probably have to be spread more thinly—
30 less money per head for food—and this may in part account for the difference in physical growth. The ability to read is closely linked to fluency in speech, and since children learn new words and expressions more by talking with adults than with other children, the time a parent can give to a child is extremely important. Fitting in well with adults, e.g. teachers, is another skill

continue overleaf

35 learnt from grown-ups. Children from large families are slower to grasp this, so they usually adjust less well to the adult standards at school.

Is the working mother a menace?

Children of working mothers usually showed no very marked effects in achievement and adjustment at school. The average loss in reading ability at
40 seven was about three months and less for arithmetic; and this was for children of full-time working mothers. These differences are not negligible but we really should stop hounding a mother merely because she works. Provided the job is not too much for her and she arranges satisfactory substitute care, the child's development almost certainly will not suffer. Children whose
45 mothers worked before they started school were no worse adjusted than children of non-working mothers. It may be that by the age of seven they were well used to the situation.

Does sex difference affect schoolwork?

Teachers reported that 71 per cent of the girls appeared very stable and
50 settled in school but only 58 per cent of the boys. Both mothers and teachers said that boys took longer to settle down. An important point here is likely to be 'sex-typed' characteristics which even by the age of seven are well formed. In our society masculinity means assertiveness (if not actual aggression), physical courage, strength and activity. However, schools clearly frown
55 upon aggression and there are limits to the amount of assertiveness they will tolerate. Although an infant school today allows—and indeed encourages— much more physical activity than twenty or thirty years ago, it still aims to be an ordered society. The robustness and restlessness of many boys must receive some check in the classroom. A boy has to adjust to school standards, which
60 in a sense are in conflict with what society is encouraging him to be. The personal characteristics that society expects in girls include a rather more passive and conforming attitude, which fits in much better with the school's demands.

Educationally, boys are just superior to girls in arithmetic at seven; they
65 are on average less than two months ahead. Girls, however, are about six months ahead in reading. Girls develop language earlier and more rapidly than boys, which probably makes it easier for them to read. They are usually less active physically, less assertive, and more conforming, which makes it more likely that they will be happy to sit down quietly with a book. Some
70 early reading material used in schools has no clear link with the world outside the home, which possibly makes the subject less interesting to boys. Arithmetic, however, is less affected by any lag in language development so that boys are not held back here. It is also more associated with the male role, so that boys would normally be more interested in learning it. This is probably
75 reinforced by the fact that number-work in most infant and primary schools involves some physical activity in the classroom and is linked increasingly with the 'real world'.

R. Davie, 'The Unequal Start',
The Sunday Times Magazine

1 The passage suggests that middle-class children are less likely to be poor readers han working-class children because they are

1 surrounded by books from their birth
2 prepared beforehand for what the schools will teach
3 sent to school at an earlier age
4 ready to behave in ways that schools desire

A 1 and 2 only
B 1 and 3 only
C 2 and 3 only
D 2 and 4 only
E 3 and 4 only

2 Working-class children who cannot settle down at school may show all of the following EXCEPT

A hostility
B minor kinds of criminal behaviour
C withdrawal
D rejection of adult standards
E depression

3 The article implies that the standards of behaviour expected in schools tend to be generally

A middle-class
B unacceptable
C aristocratic
D unchanging
E working-class

4 According to the passage, the conditions most favouring a child's success at school by the age of seven include all of the following EXCEPT

A being a member of a small family
B having frequent conversation with adults
C being born of middle-class parents
D having a bathroom not shared with other families
E being older than the others in the class

5 Which of the following is nearest in meaning to 'attainment' as it is used in line 15?

A Involvement
B Behaviour
C Accomplishment
D Cleverness
E Ambition

continue overleaf

6 The reason that seven-year-old children living in bad housing conditions generally do less well at school may be that

1   they suffer in their health
2   their friends tease them about being dirty
3   they feel isolated from those who are better off
4   their parents become depressed and irritable
5   they are often late through having to wait their turn

A   1, 2 and 3 only
B   1, 3 and 4 only
C   1, 4 and 5 only
D   2, 3 and 5 only
E   2, 4 and 5 only

7 A seven-year-old child from a small family compared with one from a large family may be all of the following EXCEPT

A   happier in temperament
B   a year ahead in reading
C   taller in stature
D   three months ahead in arithmetic
E   better attuned to school life

8 According to the article, the closer contacts with adults that seven-year-olds in small families have resulted in their

1   having a wider vocabulary
2   being better at solving problems
3   being easily adaptable to adult standards
4   having less respect for their elders

A   1 and 2 only
B   1 and 3 only
C   2 and 3 only
D   2 and 4 only
E   3 and 4 only

9 According to the passage, seven-year-olds in large families may have less

1   time to play
2   contact with their parents
3   food to eat
4   contact with their teachers

A   1 and 2 only
B   1 and 3 only
C   2 and 3 only
D   2 and 4 only
E   3 and 4 only

10 At school a seven-year-old child whose mother works full-time

    1   suffers no loss of ability to read
    2   has great difficulty in settling down
    3   suffers some loss of ability in arithmetic
    4   has only the usual problems in settling down

    A   1 and 2 only
    B   1 and 3 only
    C   2 and 3 only
    D   2 and 4 only
    E   3 and 4 only

11 The article implies that mothers who work are

    A   better-off than others
    B   indifferent about their children
    C   exhausted by their work
    D   disapproved of by society
    E   happier than other parents

12 The article suggests that seven-year-olds whose mothers have been working full-time for two years or more are

    A   accustomed to the situation
    B   very disturbed
    C   more demanding of attention
    D   rather dull
    E   able to look after themselves

13 In general, boys take longer to settle down at school than girls because schools

    A   are not properly equipped for boys to learn quickly
    B   have many more women teachers than men who are qualified
    C   teach the kinds of subjects only girls enjoy
    D   disapprove of some of their behaviour encouraged by society
    E   force boys to sit still all day long at their desks

14 The article implies that all the following are regarded by schools as desirable qualities in male behaviour EXCEPT

    1   courage
    2   assertiveness
    3   strength
    4   aggressiveness

    A   1 and 2 only
    B   1 and 3 only
    C   2 and 3 only
    D   2 and 4 only
    E   3 and 4 only

continue overleaf

15 According to the article, infant schools twenty or thirty years ago

   A had many more girls than boys
   B lacked firm internal discipline
   C put less stress on being active physically
   D emphasised arithmetic for boys and language for girls
   E had as much trouble with girls as with boys

16 In general, girls are said to settle down better at school than boys because

   A they are more sensitive than boys in most things
   B their social conditioning has always helped them conform
   C they are keener than boys to take on all forms of work
   D their later lives are more competitive than boys'
   E they can all read by the time they start school

17 It appears that generally by the age of seven

   1 boys are better behaved than girls
   2 girls are better than boys at reading
   3 girls are better than boys at games
   4 boys are better than girls at arithmetic

   A 1 and 2 only
   B 1 and 3 only
   C 2 and 3 only
   D 2 and 4 only
   E 3 and 4 only

18 Girls of seven are generally more ready than boys to read for all of the following reasons EXCEPT that they are

   A less active physically
   B more developed in language skills
   C less discriminating
   D more willing to conform
   E less assertive

19 Boys of seven are more interested than girls of the same age in arithmetic for all of the following reasons EXCEPT that they

   A feel that arithmetic is useful in sport
   B need to use language less in solving problems
   C see a link between arithmetic and life outside school
   D can be more physically active during arithmetic lessons
   E associate arithmetic with society's view of manliness

20 Which of the following factors is likely to affect a child's development at school THE LEAST?

    A   The size of the child's family

    B   A child's sex

    C   The child's mother going out to work

    D   A child's housing conditions

    E   The social class to which the child belongs

Now go back and check your work

Development

Discussion

How can people be given more chance of being equal in our society?
What part should teachers play in deciding a pupil's future career?
Mistakes parents make in bringing up their children.

Written work

The odd child out.
In what ways can Britain's housing and population problems be solved?
People I remember in my primary school.
What my family will be like when I am a parent.

Project

Local facilities (recreational, religious, etc.) for children up to the age of seven.

The hour of attack had been fixed by the staff much earlier than the infantry
wanted or thought suitable. The night had passed, as such nights often do,
shelling being less than was expected, silent altogether at times.

5   I suppose it was about three when I shook hands with Colonel Millward,
mounted the black-oozing steps of battle headquarters in the burrows below
Bilge Street, and got into the assembly trench with my signallers. It was thick
darkness and slippery going but we used an old road part of the way. Where
we lay, there were in the darkness several shattered tree-stumps above; they
seemed friendly ghosts watching the proceedings. A runner came round dis-
10   tributing our watches, which had been synchronized at Bilge Street. At 3.50,
if I am right, shortly after Vidler had passed me growling epigrams at some
recent shellbursts which had covered him with mud, the British guns spoke;
a flooded Amazon of steel flowed, roaring immensely fast over our heads, and
the machine-gun bullets made a pattern of sharper purpose and maniac
15   language against that diluvian rush. Flaring lights, small ones, great ones,
flew up and went spinning sideways into the cloud of night; one's eyes seemed
not quick enough; one heard nothing from one's shouting neighbour, and
only by the quality of the noise and flame did I know that the German shells
crashing among the tree stumps were big ones and practically on top of us.
20   We rose, scrambled ahead, found No Man's Land a comparatively good
surface, were amazed at the puny tags and rags of once multiplicative German
wire, and blundered over the once feared trench behind them without seeing
that it was a trench. Good men as they were, my party was almost half-
stunned by the unearthliness of our own barrage and when two were wounded
25   it was left to me to bandage them in my ineffective way. The dark began to
dilute itself into daylight, and as we went on we saw concrete emplacements,
apparently unattended to as yet, which had to be treated with care and
suspicion.

We still went ahead, and the mist whitened into dawn; through it came
30   running a number of Germans—a momentary doubt; we prepared for a fight;
no—'Prisoners!' shouted my batman. I went on to see all that the mist allowed;
there were troops of our Brigade advancing through the lines of men who
were beginning to consolidate the shellholes, and with map before me I
could recognize some of the places which we had certainly captured. It
35   seemed marvellous, for a moment. All ours—all these German trenches. But
stay—even now a pity looks one in the face, for these trenches are mostly

mere hedges of brushwood, hurdles, work for a sheepfold, with a shallow
ditch behind; and they have been taking our weeks of gunfire in these!

40 Another storm, and a more serious and incontestable one, was now creep-
ing on miserably with grey vapour of rain over the whole field. It was one of
the many which caused the legend, not altogether dismissed by junior officers,
that the Germans could make it rain when they wanted to. Now, too, we were
half certain that the attack had failed further on, and one more brilliant hope,
expressed a few hours before in shouts of joy, sank into the mud.

45 It was wet and it was cold. The marvel was that the day wore on, so heavy
it was; and yet the day wore on.

Edmund Blunden, *Undertones of War*

1 The first sentence of the passage suggests that the front-line soldiers

    A   did not share their leaders' opinions
    B   complained selfishly to everyone
    C   were convinced the attack would fail
    D   were full of hate for friend and foe
    E   were on the point of rising in mutiny

2 The steps are described as 'black-oozing' (line 5) probably because the soldiers'
feet

    A   covered them with mud from the trenches
    B   squeezed out dirty water from the wood and earth
    C   left dark, dirty footmarks on each plank
    D   disturbed the black fungus growing there
    E   splashed up the muddy puddles lying about

3 'Burrows' (line 5) suggest that the soldiers were

    A   engineers enjoying living in the trenches
    B   like rats killing and destroying ruthlessly
    C   troops living in rain-soaked fox-holes
    D   like rabbits living safely under the ground
    E   doomed men who have dug their own graves

4 The trees are compared with 'friendly ghosts' (line 9) because they are all of the
following EXCEPT

    A   really quite dead
    B   seen at night
    C   weird in shape
    D   sharing their waiting
    E   vaguely moving about

continue overleaf

5 Which of the following is nearest in meaning to 'synchronized' as it is used in line 10?

   A Started
   B Checked
   C Coordinated
   D Compared
   E Set

6 The phrase 'growling epigrams' (line 11) suggests that Vidler was

   A swearing and cursing in a bad-tempered voice
   B making pithy remarks in a deep, low voice
   C composing poems in a mock-serious voice
   D hurling defiance at the enemy at the top of his voice
   E shouting war slogans in a bear-like voice

7 The shells flying overhead are compared with 'a flooded Amazon' (line 13) because they

   A go relentlessly on over a broad front
   B swirl in fierce eddies above the trench
   C advance pitilessly like fierce female warriors
   D cannot be stopped at any point
   E kill everything indiscriminately

8 'Diluvian rush' (line 15) refers to

   A 'some recent shellbursts' (lines 11–12)
   B 'a flooded Amazon of steel' (line 13)
   C 'the machine-gun bullets' (line 14)
   D 'flaring lights' (line 15)
   E 'German shells' (line 18)

9 'Multiplicative' (line 21) means that the enemy wire had once been

   A thickly entangled
   B heavy to lift
   C neatly patterned
   D barbed and dangerous
   E firmly staked

10 The author's impressions of the attack on the German lines included all of the following EXCEPT

   A spinning flares
   B deafening noises
   C falling shells
   D running prisoners
   E agonising pain

11 'Blundered' (line 22) suggests that the attackers

    A   came upon the German trench unexpectedly
    B   did not know where they were expected to go
    C   fell into the trench but climbed out again
    D   took no notice of enemy opposition
    E   jumped over the trench to the far side

12 'The dark began to dilute itself into daylight' (lines 25–6) means essentially that

    A   the sun rose above the horizon dramatically
    B   it gradually grew less dark and misty than it had been
    C   darkness was suddenly replaced by light
    D   it began to rain as dawn came after the night
    E   the morning arrived clouded in a thick mist

13 'Unattended to' (line 27) suggests mainly that the concrete emplacements had been

    A   unexamined by the British
    B   deserted by the Germans
    C   unrepaired by the British
    D   unfinished by the Germans
    E   unguarded by the British

14 The concrete emplacements 'had to be treated with care and suspicion' (lines 27–8) because they

    A   were in a very dangerous condition
    B   had been built by the enemy
    C   were possibly occupied by Germans
    D   had escaped the heavy shelling
    E   were needed for use by the British

15 The British soldiers had 'a momentary doubt' (line 30) because they thought that the Germans might be

    A   giving themselves up as prisoners
    B   preparing trenches ready for an attack
    C   trying to escape by running away
    D   mounting a strong counter-attack
    E   attempting to infiltrate their lines

continue overleaf

16 The men who were 'beginning to consolidate the shellholes' (line 33) were mainly engaged in

1 filling in the deep craters
2 linking them together into a network
3 preparing them as defensive positions
4 turning them into underground burrows

A 1 and 2 only
B 1 and 3 only
C 2 and 3 only
D 2 and 4 only
E 3 and 4 only

17 The phrase 'for a moment' (line 35) added to its sentence suggests that the writer was

A disappointed
B afraid
C exhausted
D pessimistic
E wounded

18 When he saw the state of the German trenches the writer's attitude was essentially one of

1 pride
2 compassion
3 satisfaction
4 admiration

A 1 and 2 only
B 1 and 3 only
C 2 and 3 only
D 2 and 4 only
E 3 and 4 only

19 Which one of the following is nearest in meaning to 'incontestable' as it is used in line 39?

A Violent
B Obvious
C Irresistible
D Threatening
E Destructive

142

20 Lines 45–6 convey an inescapable feeling of

   A elation
   B fulfilment
   C relief
   D disillusion
   E hate

Now go back and check your work

Development

Further reading
E. M. Remarque's *All Quiet on the Western Front* shows the sadness and
waste of war from the point of view of a German soldier. It has been made
into a film which is a classic of the cinema. Jaroslav Hasek's book *The Good
Soldier Schweik* is an amusing account of a man who finds himself a soldier
and cannot adapt himself readily to the situation. See also Test Six for further
reading ideas.

Written work
Why are young people finding the idea of war more unacceptable than other
generations have found it?
What justification can you find for the ordinary man to take part in a war?
How can you explain that national enemies of thirty years ago are now
national friends?

Projects
A great general (e.g. Napoleon, Wellington, Eisenhower, Rommel, Zhukov).
Economic causes of war.
Inventions that developed during wars and which are useful to mankind.

ACKNOWLEDGMENTS

For permission to use copyright material in this book, the authors and publishers wish to thank the following: the trustees for the copyright of the late Dylan Thomas and J. M. Dent and Sons Ltd for an extract from 'A Visit to Grandpa's' (from *Portrait of the Artist as a Young Dog*) by Dylan Thomas; René Cutforth for an extract adapted from 'The Night of the Stink Bugs' (*The Listener*, 6 January 1972); Nigel Calder for an extract from 'Earthquakes' (*Observer Magazine*, 13 February 1972); Barrie and Jenkins for an extract from *Bury My Heart at Wounded Knee* by Dee Brown; Times Newspapers Ltd for extracts from 'Two Thoughts of School' by Susan Barnes (*Sunday Times Magazine* 5 December 1971) and 'Only Two can Pay' by Jane Alexander (*Sunday Times Magazine*, 12 September 1971); Faber and Faber Ltd and the owner of the copyright for the poem 'A Working Party' from the *Collected Poems* of Siegfried Sassoon; the *New Statesman* for the poem 'High Wood' by Philip Johnstone (from *The Nation*); *New Society*, the weekly review of the social sciences, 128 Long Acre, London WC2, and the authors for extracts from 'As Good as a Tonic' by Jane Alexander, 'A Street in London' by Gillian Tindall and 'The Public's Library' by Ruth Brandon; Laurence Pollinger, The Bodley Head and William Heinemann for an extract from 'The Case for the Defence' by Graham Greene (from *Collected Stories*); the *Daily Telegraph Magazine* for an extract from 'Is Breathing Dangerous?' by M. O'Donnell (28 May 1971); Bob Houlton for an extract from 'My Apprenticeship' (*The Listener*, 7 October 1971); A. D. Peters and Co. and Victor Gollancz for an extract from 'The Lament' by Liam O'Flaherty (from *Short Stories*); Seamus Heaney for an extract from 'A Poet's Childhood' (*The Listener*, 11 November 1971); George Allen and Unwin Ltd for an extract from *The Kon Tiki Expedition* by Thor Heyerdahl; Transworld Feature Syndicate Inc. for an extract from 'How many cars can Britain take?' by P. Llewellyn (*Observer Magazine*, 17 October 1971); Messrs Macdonald, London, for an extract from *Sinister Street* by Compton Mackenzie; Messrs Longman for an extract from 'The Unequal Start' by R. Davie (from *From Birth to Seven*); A. D. Peters and Co. and Oxford University Press for an extract from *Undertones of War* by Edmund Blunden.

ANSWERS

Test

	1	2	3	4	5	6	7	8	9	10
1	C	A	A	B	D	C	D	A	D	C
2	B	E	B	C	C	D	C	B	D	D
3	C	C	E	C	C	C	B	A	C	C
4	E	C	C	D	B	E	E	D	E	E
5	B	B	D	A	A	A	A	E	A	D
6	B	B	B	D	B	B	B	D	A	A
7	E	A	E	B	E	D	D	B	B	E
8	A	C	D	C	C	A	B	A	C	C
9	D	D	D	D	D	C	C	A	E	B
10	D	D	D	A	C	A	B	C	A	A
11	E	B	C	E	A	B	D	B	D	B
12	B	C	A	E	D	B	C	A	B	B
13	A	D	B	C	B	A	C	E	D	C
14	A	E	E	D	C	E	E	B	A	E
15	D	E	E	C	E	A	A	D	A	D
16	E	A	A	D	E	D	B	E	D	E
17	B	D	B	E	E	E	E	C	E	D
18	E	A	C	B	D	E	D	D	C	B
19	D	D	B	A	A	B	C	A	B	B
20	C	C	C	E	B	D	A	C	C	A

Test

	11	12	13	14	15	16	17	18	19	20
1	B	B	B	B	E	B	A	A	D	A
2	C	E	E	E	E	B	B	E	B	B
3	D	A	B	C	B	A	C	D	A	D
4	C	D	A	D	A	E	D	D	E	E
5	A	A	E	A	B	C	E	E	C	C
6	E	D	A	D	D	C	A	D	B	B
7	D	A	C	C	C	D	D	B	A	A
8	A	D	D	B	B	C	B	E	B	B
9	B	B	B	A	A	E	D	C	C	A
10	A	C	D	C	C	E	C	C	E	E
11	A	D	E	D	D	D	E	D	D	A
12	E	B	E	E	E	D	D	A	A	B
13	C	B	D	D	E	A	A	C	D	A
14	E	C	B	B	C	E	C	B	D	C
15	C	A	A	E	D	C	E	B	C	D
16	E	E	B	E	A	B	C	B	B	B
17	B	C	C	C	D	D	B	A	D	D
18	E	E	C	A	A	B	E	C	C	D
19	A	A	B	E	D	E	E	E	A	C
20	C	C	C	D	B	C	B	E	C	D